HARRIET
BEECHER STOWE

HOUSE AND HOME PAPERS

APPLEWOOD BOOKS
Carlisle, Massachusetts

House and Home Papers was originally published in 1865.

ISBN: 978-1-4290-9743-7

Prepared for Publication by HP

MRS. STOWE'S WRITINGS.

HOUSE AND HOME PAPERS.
One Volume.

THE PEARL OF ORR'S ISLAND.
One Volume.

AGNES OF SORRENTO.
One Volume.

UNCLE TOM'S CABIN.
One Volume.

THE MINISTER'S WOOING.
One Volume.

TICKNOR AND FIELDS, Publishers.

HOUSE AND HOME

PAPERS.

By CHRISTOPHER CROWFIELD.

BOSTON:
TICKNOR AND FIELDS.
1865.

UNIVERSITY PRESS:
WELCH, BIGELOW, AND COMPANY,
CAMBRIDGE.

CONTENTS.

HOUSE AND HOME PAPERS.

I.

THE RAVAGES OF A CARPET.

"MY dear, it's so cheap!"

These words were spoken by my wife, as she sat gracefully on a roll of Brussels carpet which was spread out in flowery lengths on the floor of Messrs. Ketchem & Co.

"It's *so* cheap!"

Milton says that the love of fame is the last infirmity of noble minds. I think he had not rightly considered the subject. I believe that last infirmity is the love of getting things cheap! Understand me, now. I don't mean the love of getting cheap things, by which one understands showy, trashy, ill-made, spurious articles, bearing certain apparent resemblances to better things. All really sensible people are quite superior to that sort of cheapness. But those fortunate accidents which put within the power of a man things really good and valuable for half or a third of their value what mortal virtue and resolu-

tion can withstand? My friend Brown has a genuine
Murillo, the joy of his heart and the light of his eyes,
but he never fails to tell you, as its crowning merit,
how he bought it in South America for just nothing,
— how it hung smoky and deserted in the back of a
counting-room, and was thrown in as a makeweight to
bind a bargain, and, upon being cleaned, turned out
a genuine Murillo; and then he takes out his cigar,
and calls your attention to the points in it; he adjusts
the curtain to let the sunlight fall just in the right
spot; he takes you to this and the other point of
view; and all this time you must confess, that, in
your mind as well as his, the consideration that he
got all this beauty for ten dollars adds lustre to the
painting. Brown has paintings there for which he
paid his thousands, and, being well advised, they are
worth the thousands he paid; but this ewe-lamb that
he got for nothing always gives him a secret exaltation
in his own eyes. He seems to have credited to himself personally merit to the amount of what he should
have paid for the picture. Then there is Mrs. Crœsus,
at the party yesterday evening, expatiating to my wife
on the surprising cheapness of her point-lace set, —
"Got for just nothing at all, my dear!" and a circle
of admiring listeners echoes the sound. "Did you
ever *hear* anything like it? I never heard of such a
thing in my life"; and away sails Mrs. Crœsus as if

she had a collar composed of all the cardinal virtues. In fact, she is buoyed up with a secret sense of merit, so that her satin slippers scarcely touch the carpet. Even I myself am fond of showing a first edition of " Paradise Lost," for which I gave a shilling in a London book-stall, and stating that I would not take a hundred dollars for it. Even I must confess there are points on which I am mortal.

But all this while my wife sits on her roll of carpet, looking into my face for approbation, and Marianne and Jenny are pouring into my ear a running-fire of " How sweet ! How lovely ! Just like that one of Mrs. Tweedleum's ! "

" And she gave two dollars and seventy-five cents a yard for hers, and this is — "

My wife here put her hand to her mouth, and pronounced the incredible sum in a whisper, with a species of sacred awe, common, as I have observed, to females in such interesting crises. In fact, Mr. Ketchem, standing smiling and amiable by, remarked to me that really he hoped Mrs. Crowfield would not name generally what she gave for the article, for positively it was so far below the usual rate of prices that he might give offence to other customers ; but this was the very last of the pattern, and they were anxious to close off the old stock, and we had always traded with them, and he had a great respect for my wife's father, who had always traded with their firm, and so, when there were any little bargains to be thrown in any one's way, why, he naturally, of course — And here Mr. Ketchem bowed gracefully over the yardstick to my wife, and I consented.

Yes, I consented; but whenever I think of myself at that moment, I always am reminded, in a small way, of Adam taking the apple; and my wife, seated on that roll of carpet, has more than once suggested to my mind the classic image of Pandora opening her unlucky box. In fact, from the moment I had blandly assented to Mr. Ketchem's remarks, and said to my wife, with a gentle air of dignity, "Well, my dear, since it suits you, I think you had better take it," there came a load on my prophetic soul, which not all the fluttering and chattering of my delighted girls and the more placid complacency of my wife could entirely dissipate. I presaged, I know not what, of coming woe; and all I presaged came to pass.

In order to know just *what* came to pass, I must give you a view of the house and home into which this carpet was introduced.

My wife and I were somewhat advanced housekeepers, and our dwelling was first furnished by her father, in the old-fashioned jog-trot days, when furniture was made with a view to its lasting from generation to generation. Everything was strong and comfortable, — heavy mahogany, guiltless of the modern device of veneering, and hewed out with a square solidity which had not an idea of change. It was, so to speak, a sort of granite foundation of the household structure. Then, we commenced housekeeping with the full idea that our house was a thing to be lived in, and that furniture was made to be used. That most sensible of women, Mrs. Crowfield, agreed fully with me, that in our house there was to be nothing too good for ourselves, — no rooms shut up in holiday attire to be enjoyed by strangers for three or four days in the year, while we lived in holes and corners, — no best parlor from which we were to be excluded, — no silver plate to be kept in the safe in the bank, and brought home only in case of a grand festival, while our daily meals were served with dingy Britannia. "Strike a broad, plain average," I said to my wife ; "have everything abundant, serviceable ; and give all our friends exactly what we have ourselves, no better and no worse" ; — and my wife smiled approval on my sentiment.

Smile ! she did more than smile. My wife resembles one of those convex mirrors I have sometimes seen. Every idea I threw out, plain and simple, she reflected back upon me in a thousand little glitters

and twinkles of her own; she made my crude conceptions come back to me in such perfectly dazzling
performances that I hardly recognized them. My
mind warms up, when I think what a home that woman made of our house from the very first day she
moved into it. The great, large, airy parlor, with its
ample bow-window, when she had arranged it, seemed
a perfect trap to catch sunbeams. There was none
of that discouraging trimness and newness that often
repel a man's bachelor-friends after the first call, and
make them feel, — "O, well, one cannot go in at
Crowfield's now, unless one is dressed; one might
put them out." The first thing our parlor said to
any one was, that we were not people to be put out,
that we were wide-spread, easy-going, and jolly folk.
Even if Tom Brown brought in Ponto and his shoot-
ing-bag, there was nothing in that parlor to strike
terror into man and dog; for it was written on the
face of things, that everybody there was to do just
as he or she pleased. There were my books and
my writing-table spread out with all its miscellaneous
confusion of papers on one side of the fireplace, and
there were my wife's great, ample sofa and work-table
on the other; there I wrote my articles for the
"North American," and there she turned and ripped
and altered her dresses, and there lay crochet and
knitting and embroidery side by side with a weekly

basket of family-mending, and in neighborly contigu-
ity with the last book of the season, which my wife
turned over as she took her after-dinner lounge on
the sofa. · And in the bow-window were canaries
always singing, and a great stand of plants always
fresh and blooming, and ivy which grew and clam-
bered and twined about the pictures. Best of all,
there was in our parlor that household altar, the
blazing wood-fire, whose wholesome, hearty crackle
is the truest household inspiration. I quite agree
with one celebrated American author who holds that
an open fireplace is an altar of patriotism. Would
our Revolutionary fathers have gone barefooted and
bleeding over snows to defend air-tight stoves and
cooking-ranges? I trow not, It was the memory of
the great open kitchen-fire, with its back-log and fore-
stick of cord-wood, its roaring, hilarious voice of
invitation, its dancing tongues of flame, that called
to them through the snows of that dreadful winter to
keep up their courage, that made their hearts warm
and bright with a thousand reflected memories. Our
neighbors said that it was delightful to sit by our fire,
—but then, for their part, they could not afford it,
wood was so ruinously dear, and all that. Most of
these people could not, for the simple reason that
they felt compelled, in order to maintain the family-
dignity, to keep up a parlor with great pomp and

circumstance of upholstery, where they sat only on dress-occasions, and of course the wood-fire was out of the question.

When children began to make their appearance in our establishment, my wife, like a well-conducted housekeeper, had the best of nursery-arrangements, — a room all warmed, lighted, and ventilated, and abounding in every proper resource of amusement to the rising race; but it was astonishing to see how, notwithstanding this, the centripetal attraction drew every pair of little pattering feet to our parlor.

"My dear, why don't you take your blocks up-stairs?"

"I want to be where oo are," said with a piteous under-lip, was generally a most convincing answer.

Then the small people could not be disabused of the idea that certain chief treasures of their own would be safer under papa's writing-table or mamma's sofa than in the safest closet of their own domains. My writing-table was dock-yard for Arthur's new ship, and stable for little Tom's pepper-and-salt-colored pony, and carriage-house for Charley's new wagon, while whole armies of paper-dolls kept house in the recess behind mamma's sofa.

And then, in due time, came the tribe of pets who followed the little ones and rejoiced in the blaze of the firelight. The boys had a splendid Newfound-

land, which, knowing our weakness, we warned them
with awful gravity was never to be a parlor dog; but,
somehow, what with little beggings and pleadings on
the part of Arthur and Tom, and the piteous melancholy with which Rover would look through the win-
dow-panes, when shut out from the blazing warmth
into the dark, cold, veranda, it at last came to pass
that Rover gained a regular corner at the hearth, a
regular *status* in every family-convocation. And then
came a little black-and-tan English terrier for the
girls; and then a fleecy poodle, who established himself on the corner of my wife's sofa; and for each of
these some little voices pleaded, and some little heart
would be so near broken at any slight, that my wife
and I resigned ourselves to live in menagerie, the more
so as we were obliged to confess a lurking weakness
towards these four-footed children ourselves.

So we grew and flourished together, — children,
dogs, birds, flowers, and all; and although my wife
often, in paroxysms of housewifeliness to which the
best of women are subject, would declare that we
never were fit to be· seen, yet I comforted her with
the reflection that there were few people whose
friends seemed to consider them better worth seeing,
judging by the stream of visitors and loungers which
was always setting towards our parlor. People
seemed to find it good to be there; they said it

was somehow home-like and pleasant, and that there
was a kind of charm about it that made it easy to
talk and easy to live; and as my girls and boys grew
up, there seemed always to be some merry doing or
other going on there.   Arty and Tom brought home
their college friends, who straightway took root there
and seemed to fancy themselves a part of us.   We
had no reception-rooms apart, where the girls were
to receive young gentlemen; all the courting and
flirting that were to be done had for their arena the
ample variety of surface presented by our parlor,
which, with sofas and screens and lounges and recesses and writing- and work-tables, disposed here
and there, and the genuine *laisser aller* of the whole
menage, seemed, on the whole, to have offered ample
advantages enough; for, at the time I write of, two
daughters were already established in marriage, while
my youngest was busy, as yet, in performing that
little domestic ballet of the cat with the mouse, in
the case of a most submissive youth of the neighborhood.

All this time our parlor-furniture, though of that
granitic formation I have indicated, began to show
marks of that decay to which things sublunary are
liable.   I cannot say that I dislike this look in a
room.   Take a fine, ample, hospitable apartment,
where all things, freely and generously used, softly

and indefinably grow old together, there is a sort of
mellow tone and keeping which pleases my eye.
What if the seams of the great inviting arm-chair,
where so many friends have sat and lounged, do grow
white? What, in fact, if some easy couch has an undeniable hole worn in its friendly cover? I regard
with tenderness even these mortal weaknesses of
these servants and witnesses of our good times and
social fellowship. No vulgar touch wore them; they
may be called, rather, the marks and indentations
which the glittering in and out of the tide of social
happiness has worn in the rocks of our strand. I
would no more disturb the gradual toning-down and
aging of a well-used set of furniture by smart improvements than I would have a modern dauber paint in
emendations in a fine old picture.

So we men reason; but women do not always
think as we do. There is a virulent demon of housekeeping, not wholly cast out in the best of them, and
which often breaks out in unguarded moments. In
fact, Miss Marianne, being on the lookout for furniture wherewith to begin a new establishment, and
Jenny, who had accompanied her in her peregrina-
tions, had more than once thrown out little dispar-
aging remarks on the time-worn appearance of our
establishment, suggesting comparison with those of
more modern-furnished rooms.

"It is positively scandalous, the way our furniture looks," I one day heard one of them declaring to her mother; "and this old rag of a carpet!"

My feelings were hurt, not the less so that I knew that the large cloth which covered the middle of the floor, and which the women call a bocking, had been bought and nailed down there, after a solemn family-counsel, as the best means of concealing the too evident darns which years of good cheer had made needful in our stanch old household friend, the three-ply carpet, made in those days when to be a three-ply was a pledge of continuance and service.

Well, it was a joyous and bustling day, when, after one of those domestic whirlwinds which the women are · fond of denominating house-cleaning, the new Brussels carpet was at length brought in and nailed down, and its beauty praised from mouth to mouth. Our old friends called in and admired, and all seemed to be well, except that I had that light and delicate presage of changes to come which indefinitely brooded over me.

The first premonitory symptom was the look of apprehensive suspicion with which the female senate regarded the genial sunbeams that had always glorified our bow-window.

"This house ought to have inside blinds," said Marianne, with all the confident decision of· youth;

"this carpet will be ruined, if the sun is allowed to come in like that."

"And that dirty little canary must really be hung in the kitchen," said Jenny; "he always did make such a litter, scattering his seed-chippings about; and he never takes his bath without flirting out some water. And, mamma, it appears to me it will never do to have the plants here. Plants are always either leaking through the pots upon the carpet, or scattering bits of blossoms and dead leaves, or some accident upsets or breaks a pot. It was no matter, you know, when we had the old carpet; but this we really want to have kept nice."

Mamma stood her ground for the plants, — darlings of her heart for many a year, — but temporized, and showed that disposition towards compromise which is most inviting to aggression.

I confess I trembled; for, of all radicals on earth, none are to be compared to females that have once in hand a course of domestic innovation and reform. The sacred fire, the divine *furor*, burns in their bosoms, they become perfect Pythonesses, and every chair they sit on assumes the magic properties of the tripod. Hence the dismay that lodges in the bosoms of us males at the fateful spring and autumn seasons, denominated house-cleaning. Who can say whither the awful gods, the prophetic fates, may drive our fair household divinities; what sins of ours may be brought to light; what indulgences and compliances, which uninspired woman has granted in her ordinary mortal hours, may be torn from us? He who has been allowed to keep a pair of pet slippers in a concealed corner, and by the fireside indulged with a chair which he might, *ad libitum*, fill with all sorts of pamphlets and miscellaneous literature, suddenly finds himself reformed out of knowledge, his pamphlets tucked away into pigeon-holes and corners, and his slippers put in their place in the hall, with, perhaps, a brisk insinuation about the shocking dust and disorder that men will tolerate.

The fact was, that the very first night after the advent of the new carpet I had a prophetic dream. Among our treasures of art was a little etching, by an English artist-friend, the subject of which was the gambols of the household fairies in a baronial library after the household were in bed. The little people are represented in every attitude of frolic enjoyment. Some escalade the great arm-chair, and look down from its top as from a domestic Mont Blanc; some climb about the bellows; some scale the shaft of the shovel; while some, forming in magic ring, dance festively on the yet glowing hearth. Tiny troops promenade the writing-table. One perches himself quaintly on the top of the inkstand, and holds colloquy with another who sits cross-legged on a paper-weight, while a companion looks down on them from the top of the sand-box. It was an ingenious little device, and gave me the idea, which I often expressed to my wife, that much of the peculiar feeling of se-curity, composure, and enjoyment which seems to be the atmosphere of some rooms and houses came from the unsuspected presence of these little people, the household fairies, so that the belief in their existence became a solemn article of faith with me.

Accordingly, that evening, after the installation of the carpet, when my wife and daughters had gone to bed, as I sat with my slippered feet before the last coals of the fire, I fell asleep in my chair, and, lo! my own parlor presented to my eye a scene of busy life. The little people in green were tripping to and fro, but in great confusion. Evidently something was wrong among them; for they were fussing and chattering with each other, as if preparatory to a gen-eral movement. In the region of the bow-window I observed a tribe of them standing with tiny valises and carpet-bags in their hands, as though about to depart on a journey. On my writing-table another set stood around my inkstand and pen-rack, who, point-ing to those on the floor, seemed to debate some question among themselves; while others of them appeared to be collecting and packing away in tiny trunks certain fairy treasures, preparatory to a general departure. When I looked at the social hearth, at my wife's sofa and work-basket, I saw similar appearances of dissatisfaction and confusion. It was evident that the household fairies were discussing the question of a general and simultaneous removal. I groaned in spirit, and, stretching out my hand, began a conciliatory address, when whisk went the whole scene from before my eyes, and I awaked to behold the form of my wife asking me if I were ill or had had the nightmare that I groaned so. I told her my dream, and we laughed at it together.

"We must give way to the girls a little," she said. "It is natural, you know, that they should wish us to appear a little as other people do. The fact is, our parlor is somewhat dilapidated; think how many years we have lived in it without an article of new furniture."

"I hate new furniture," I remarked, in the bitterness of my soul. "I hate anything new."

My wife answered me discreetly, according to approved principles of diplomacy. I was right. She sympathized with me. At the same time, it was not necessary, she remarked, that we should keep a hole in our sofa-cover and arm-chair; there would certainly be no harm in sending them to the upholsterer's to be new-covered; she did n't much mind, for her part, moving her plants to the south back-room, and the bird would do well enough in the kitchen : I had often complained of him for singing vociferously when I was reading aloud.

So our sofa went to the upholsterer's ; but the upholsterer was struck with such horror at its clumsy, antiquated, unfashionable appearance, that he felt bound to make representations to my wife and daughters : positively, it would be better for them to get a new one, of a tempting pattern, which he showed them, than to try to do anything with that. With a stitch or so here and there it might do for a basement dining-room ; but, for a parlor, he gave it as his disinterested opinion, — he must say, if the case were his own, he should get, etc., etc. In short, we had a new sofa and new chairs, and the plants and the birds were banished, and some dark green blinds were put up to exclude the sun from the parlor, and the blessed luminary was allowed there only at rare intervals, when my wife and daughters were out shopping, and I acted out my uncivilized male instincts by pulling up every shade and vivifying the apartment as in days of old.

But this was not the worst of it. The new furniture and new carpet formed an opposition party in the room. I believe in my heart that for every little household fairy that went out with the dear old things there came in a tribe of discontented brownies with

B

the new ones. These little wretches were always
twitching at the gowns of my wife and daughters, jog-
ging their elbows, and suggesting odious comparisons
between the smart new articles and what remained of
the old ones. They disparaged my writing-table in
the corner ; they disparaged the old-fashioned lounge
in the other corner, which had been the maternal
throne for years ; they disparaged the work-table, the
work-basket, with constant suggestions of how such
things as these would look in certain well-kept parlors
where new-fashioned furniture of the same sort as
ours existed.

"We don't have any parlor," said Jenny, one day.
"Our parlor has always been a sort of log-cabin, —
library, study, nursery, greenhouse, all combined. We
never have had things like other people."

"Yes, and this open fire makes such a dust ; and
this carpet is one that shows every speck of dust ; it
keeps one always on the watch."

"I wonder why papa never had a study to himself ;
I 'm sure I should think he would like it better than
sitting here among us all. Now there 's the great
south-room off the dining-room ; if he would only
move his things there, and have his open fire, we
could then close up the fireplace, and put lounges in
the recesses, and mamma could have her things in the
nursery, — and then we should have a parlor fit to be
seen."

I overheard all this, though I pretended not to, —
the little busy chits supposing me entirely buried in
the recesses of a German book over which I was
poring.

There are certain crises in a man's life when the
female element in his household asserts itself in domi-
nant forms that seem to threaten to overwhelm him.
The fair creatures, who in most matters have depended
on his judgment, evidently look upon him at these
seasons as only a forlorn, incapable male creature, to
be cajoled and flattered and persuaded out of his
native blindness and absurdity into the fairy-land of
their wishes.

"Of course, mamma," said the busy voices, "men
can't understand such things. What *can* men know of
housekeeping, and how things ought to look? Papa
never goes into company; he don't know and don't
care how the world is doing, and don't see that nobody now is living as we do."

"Aha, my little mistresses, are you there?" I
thought; and I mentally resolved on opposing a
great force of what our politicians call *backbone* to
this pretty domestic conspiracy.

"When you get my writing-table out of this corner,
my pretty dears, I'd thank you to let me know it."

Thus spake I in my blindness, fool that I was.
Jupiter might as soon keep awake, when Juno came

in best bib and tucker, and with the *cestus* of Venus,
to get him to sleep. Poor Slender might as well hope
to get the better of pretty Mistress Anne Page, as one
of us clumsy-footed men might endeavor to escape
from the tangled labyrinth of female wiles.

In short, in less than a year it was all done, without
any quarrel, any noise, any violence, — done, I scarce
knew when or how, but with the utmost deference to
my wishes, the most amiable hopes that I would not
put myself out, the most sincere protestations that, if
I liked it better as it was, my goddesses would give
up and acquiesce. In fact, I seemed to do it of myself, constrained thereto by what the Emperor Napoleon has so happily called the logic of events, — that
old, well-known logic by which the man who has once
said A must say B, and he who has said B must say
the whole alphabet. In a year, we had a parlor with
two lounges in decorous recesses, a fashionable sofa,
and six chairs and a looking-glass, and a grate always
shut up, and a hole in the floor which kept the parlor
warm, and great, heavy curtains that kept out all the
light that was not already excluded by the green
shades.

It was as proper and orderly a parlor as those of
our most fashionable neighbors ; and when our friends
called, we took them stumbling into its darkened solitude, and opened a faint crack in one of the window-

shades, and came down in our best clothes, and talked
with them there. Our old friends rebelled at this,
and asked what they had done to be treated so, and
complained so bitterly that gradually we let them into
the secret that there was a great south-room which I
had taken for my study, where we all sat, where the
old carpet was down, where the sun shone in at the
great window, where my wife's plants flourished and
the canary-bird sang, and my wife had her sofa in the
corner, and the old brass andirons glistened and the
wood-fire crackled, — in short, a room to which all the
household fairies had emigrated.

When they once had found *that* out, it was difficult
to get any of them to sit in our parlor. I had pur-
posely christened the new room *my study*, that I might
stand on my rights as master of ceremonies there,
though I opened wide arms of welcome to any who
chose to come. So, then, it would often come to pass,
that, when we were sitting round the fire in my study
of an evening, the girls would say, —

"Come, what do we always stay here for? Why
don't we ever sit in the parlor?"

And then there would be manifested among guests
and family-friends a general unwillingness to move.

"O, hang it, girls!" would Arthur say; "the parlor
is well enough, all right; let it stay as it is, and let
a fellow stay where he can do as he pleases and feels

at home "; and to this view of the matter would respond divers of the nice young bachelors who were Arthur's and Tom's sworn friends.

In fact, nobody wanted to stay in our parlor now. It was a cold, correct, accomplished fact ; the household fairies had left it, — and when the fairies leave a room, nobody ever feels at home in it.   No pictures, curtains, no wealth of mirrors, no elegance of lounges, can in the least make up for their absence.   They are a capricious little set ; there are rooms where they will *not* stay, and rooms where they *will;* but no one can ever have a good time without them.

II.

HOME–KEEPING *vs.* HOUSE–KEEPING.

I AM a frank, open-hearted man, as, perhaps, you have by this time perceived, and you will not, therefore, be surprised to know that I read my last article on the carpet to my wife and the girls before I sent it to the "Atlantic," and we had a hearty laugh over it together. My wife and the girls, in fact, felt that they could afford to laugh, for they had carried their point, their reproach among women was taken away, they had become like other folks. Like other folks they had a parlor, an undeniable best parlor,. shut up and darkened, with all proper carpets, curtains, lounges, and marble-topped tables, too good for human nature's daily food ; and being sustained by this consciousness, they cheerfully went on receiving their friends in the study, and having good times in the old free-and-easy way ; for did not everybody know that this room was not their best ? and if the furniture was old-fashioned and a little the worse for antiquity, was it not certain that they had better, which they could use, if they would ?

"And supposing we wanted to give a party," said Jenny, "how nicely our parlor would light up ! Not that we ever do give parties, but if we should, — and for a wedding-reception, you know."

I felt the force of the necessity ; it was evident that the four or five hundred extra which we had expended was no more than such solemn possibilities required.

"Now, papa thinks we have been foolish," said Marianne, "and he has his own way of making a good story of it ; but, after all, I desire to know if people are never to get a new carpet. Must we keep the old one till it actually wears to tatters ?"

This is a specimen of the *reductio ad absurdum* which our fair antagonists of the other sex are fond of employing. They strip what we say of all delicate shadings and illusory phrases, and reduce it to some bare question of fact, with which they make a home-thrust at us.

"Yes, that's it ; are people *never* to get a new carpet ?" echoed Jenny.

"My dears," I replied, "it is a fact that to introduce anything new into an apartment hallowed by many home-associations, where all things have grown old together, requires as much care and adroitness as for an architect to restore an arch or niche in a fine old ruin. The fault of our carpet was that it was in another style from everything in our room, and made everything in it look dilapidated. Its colors, material, and air belonged to another manner of life, and were a constant plea for alterations ; and you see it actually drove out and expelled the whole furniture of the room, and I am not sure yet that it may not entail on us the necessity of refurnishing the whole house."

" My dear !" said my wife, in a tone of remonstrance ; but Jane and Marianne laughed and colored.

"Confess, now," said I, looking at them, "have you not had secret designs on the hall- and stair-carpet ? "

" Now, papa, how could you know it ? I only said to Marianne that to have Brussels in the parlor and that old mean-looking ingrain carpet in the hall did not seem exactly the thing ; and, in fact, you know, mamma, Messrs. Ketchem & Co. showed us such a lovely pattern, designed to harmonize with our parlor-carpet."

" I know it, girls," said my wife ; "but you know I said at once that such an expense was not to be thought of."

" Now, girls," said I, " let me tell you a story I heard once of a very sensible old New England minister, who lived, as our country ministers generally do, rather near to the bone, but still quite contentedly. It

2

was in the days when knee-breeches and long stock-
ings were worn, and this good man was offered a
present of a very nice pair of black silk hose. He
declined, saying, he 'could not afford to wear them.'

"'Not afford it?' said the friend; 'why, I *give*
them to you.'

"'Exactly; but it will cost me not less than two
hundred dollars to take them, and I cannot do it.'

"'How is that?'

"'Why, in the first place, I shall no sooner put
them on than my wife will say, "My dear, you must
have a new pair of knee-breeches," and I shall get
them. Then my wife will say, "My dear, how
shabby your coat is! You must have a new one,"
and I shall get a new coat. Then she will say,
"Now, my dear, that hat will never do," and then
I shall have a new hat; and then I shall say, "My
dear, it will never do for me to be so fine and you to
wear your old gown," and so my wife will get a new
gown; and then the new gown will require a new
shawl and a new bonnet; all of which we shall not
feel the need of, if I don't take this pair of silk stock-
ings, for, as long as we don't see them, our old things
seem very well suited to each other.'"

The girls laughed at this story, and I then added,
in my most determined manner, —

"But I must warn you, girls, that I have compro-

mised to the utmost extent of my power, and that I
intend to plant myself on the old stair-carpet in determined resistance. I have no mind to be forbidden
the use of the front-stairs, or condemned to get up
into my bedroom by a private ladder, as I should be
immediately, if there were a new carpet down."

" Why, papa ! "

"Would it not be so ? Can the sun shine in the
parlor now for fear of fading the carpet ? Can we
keep a fire there for fear of making dust, or use the
lounges and sofas for fear of wearing them out ? If
you got a new entry- and stair-carpet, as I said, I
should have to be at the expense of another staircase to get up to our bedroom."

"O no, papa," said Jane, innocently ; "there are
very pretty druggets, now, for covering stair-carpets,
so that they can be used without hurting them."

" Put one over the old carpet, then," said I, " and
our acquaintance will never know but it is a new
one."

All the female senate laughed at this proposal, and
said it sounded just like a man.

"Well," said I, standing up resolutely for my sex,
"a man's ideas on woman's matters may be worth
some attention. I flatter myself that an intelligent,
educated man does n't think upon and observe with
interest any particular subject for years of his life

without gaining some ideas respecting it that are good for something ; at all events, I have written another article for the 'Atlantic,' which I will read to you."

"Well, wait one minute, papa, till we get our work," said the girls, who, to say the truth, always exhibit a flattering interest in anything their papa writes, and who have the good taste never to interrupt his readings with any conversations in an undertone on cross-stitch and floss-silks, as the manner of some is. Hence the little feminine bustle of arranging all these matters beforehand. Jane, or Jenny, as I call her in my good-natured moods, put on a fresh clear stick of hickory, of that species denominated shagbark, which is full of most charming slivers, burning with such a clear flame, and emitting such a delicious perfume in burning, that I would not change it with the millionnaire who kept up his fire with cinnamon.

You must know, my dear Mr. Atlantic, and you, my confidential friends of the reading public, that there is a certain magic or spiritualism which I have the knack of in regard to these mine articles, in virtue of which my wife and daughters never hear or see the little personalities respecting *them* which form parts of my papers. By a peculiar arrangement which I have made with the elves of the inkstand and the familiar spirits of the quill, a sort of glamour falls on their eyes and ears when I am reading, or when they read the parts personal to themselves; otherwise their sense of feminine propriety would be shocked at the free way in which they and their most internal affairs are confidentially spoken of between me and you, O loving readers.

Thus, in an undertone, I tell you that my little Jenny, as she is zealously and systematically arranging the fire, and trimly whisking every untidy particle of ashes from the hearth, shows in every movement of her little hands, in the cock of her head, in the knowing, observing glance of her eye, and in all her energetic movements, that her small person is endued and made up of the very expressed essence of house-wifeliness, — she is the very attar, not of roses, but of housekeeping. Care-taking and thrift and neatness are a nature to her; she is as dainty and delicate in her person as a white cat, as everlastingly busy as a bee; and all the most needful faculties of time, weight, measure, and proportion ought to be fully developed in her skull, if there is any truth in phrenology. Besides all this, she has a sort of hard-grained little vein of common sense, against which my fanciful conceptions and poetical notions are apt to hit with just a little sharp grating, if they are not well put. In fact, this kind of woman needs carefully to be idealized in the process of education, or she will stiffen and dry, as she grows old, into a veritable household Pharisee, a sort of domestic tyrant. She needs to be trained in artistic values and artistic weights and measures, to study all the arts and sciences of the beautiful, and then she is charming. Most useful, most needful, these little women : they have the centripetal force which keeps all the domestic planets from gyrating and frisking in unseemly orbits,— and properly trained, they fill a house with the beauty of order, the harmony and consistency of proportion, the melody of things moving in time and tune, without violating the graceful appearance of ease which Art requires.

So I had an eye to Jenny's education in my article which I unfolded and read, and which was entitled,

HOME-KEEPING *vs.* HOUSE-KEEPING.

THERE are many women who know how to keep a house, but there are but few that know how to keep a *home.* To keep a house may seem a complicated affair, but it is a thing that may be learned ; it lies in the region of the material, in the region of weight, measure, color, and the positive forces of life. To keep a home lies not merely in the sphere of all these, but it takes in the intellectual, the social, the spiritual, the immortal.

Here the hickory-stick broke in two, and the two

brands fell controversially out and apart on the hearth, scattering the ashes and coals, and calling for Jenny and the hearth-brush. Your wood-fire has this foible, that it needs something to be done to it every five minutes; but, after all, these little interruptions of our bright-faced genius are like the piquant sallies of a clever friend, — they do not strike us as unreasonable.

When Jenny had laid down her brush, she said, —

" Seems to me, papa, you are beginning to soar into metaphysics."

" Everything in creation is metaphysical in its abstract terms," said I, with a look calculated to reduce her to a respectful condition. " Everything has a subjective and an objective mode of presentation."

" There papa goes with subjective and objective ! " said Marianne. " For my part, I never can remember which is which."

" I remember," said Jenny ; " it 's what our old nurse used to call internal and *out*-ternal, — I always remember by that."

" Come, my dears," said my wife, " let your father read " ; so I went on as follows : —

I remember in my bachelor days going with my boon companion, Bill Carberry, to look at the house to which he was in a few weeks to introduce his bride.

Bill was a gallant, free-hearted, open-handed fellow, the life of our whole set, and we felt that natural aversion to losing him that bachelor friends would. How could we tell under what strange aspects he might look forth upon us, when once he had passed into "that undiscovered country" of matrimony? But Bill laughed to scorn our apprehensions.

"I 'll tell you what, Chris," he said, as he sprang cheerily up the steps and unlocked the door of his future dwelling, "do you know what I chose this house for? Because it 's a social-looking house. Look there, now," he said, as he ushered me into a pair of parlors, — "look at those long south windows, the sun lies there nearly all day long; see what a capital corner there is for a lounging-chair; fancy us, Chris, with our books or our paper, spread out loose and easy, and Sophie gliding in and out like a sunbeam. I 'm getting poetical, you see. Then, did you ever see a better, wider, airier dining-room? What capital suppers and things we 'll have there! the nicest times, — everything free and easy, you know, — just what I 've always wanted a house for. I tell you, Chris, you and Tom Innis shall have latch-keys just like mine, and there is a capital chamber there at the head of the stairs, so that you can be free to come and go. And here now 's the library, — fancy this full of books and engravings from the ceiling to the floor; here you

shall come just as you please and ask no questions, —
all the same as if it were your own, you know."

" And Sophie, what will she say to all this ? "

" Why, you know Sophie is a prime friend to both
of you, and a capital girl to keep things going. O,
Sophie 'll make a house of this, you may depend ! "

A day or two after, Bill dragged me stumbling over
boxes and through straw and wrappings to show me
the glories of the parlor-furniture, — with which he
seemed pleased as a child with a new toy.

" Look here," he said ; " see these chairs, garnet-
colored satin, with a pattern on each ; well, the sofa 's
just like them, and the curtains to match, and the
carpets made for the floor with centre-pieces and
borders. I never saw anything more magnificent in
my life. Sophie's governor furnishes the house, and
everything is to be A No. 1, and all that, you see.
Messrs. Curtain and Collamore are coming to make
the rooms up, and her mother is busy as a bee getting
us in order."

" Why, Bill," said I, " you are going to be lodged
like a prince. I hope you 'll be able to keep it up ;
but law-business comes in rather slowly at first, old
fellow."

" Well, you know it is n't the way I should furnish,
if my capital was the one to cash the bills ; but then,
you see, Sophie's people do it, and let them, — a girl

2 *   c

does n't want to come down out of the style she has always lived in."

I said nothing, but had an oppressive presentiment that social freedom would expire in that house, crushed under a weight of upholstery.

But there came in due time the wedding and the wedding-reception, and we all went to see Bill in his new house splendidly lighted up and complete from top to toe, and everybody said what a lucky fellow he was ; but that was about the end of it, so far as our visiting was concerned. The running in, and dropping in, and keeping latch-keys, and making informal calls, that had been forespoken, seemed about as likely as if Bill had lodged in the Tuileries. ·

Sophie, who had always been one of your snapping, sparkling, busy sort of girls, began at once to develop her womanhood, and show her principles, and was as different from her former self as your careworn, mousing old cat is from your rollicking, frisky kitten. Not but that Sophie was a good girl. She had a capital heart, a good, true womanly one, and was loving and obliging ; but still she was one of the desperately painstaking, conscientious sort of women whose very blood, as they grow older, is devoured with anxiety, and she came of a race of women in whom housekeeping was more than an art or a science, — it was, so to speak, a religion. Sophie's mother, aunts, and grandmothers, for nameless generations back, were known and celebrated housekeepers. They might have been genuine descendants of the inhabitants of that Hollandic town of Broeck, celebrated by Washington Irving, where the cows' tails are kept tied up with unsullied blue ribbons, and the ends of the firewood are painted white. He relates how a celebrated preacher, visiting this town, found it impossible to draw these housewives from their earthly views and employments, until he took to preaching on the *neatness* of the celestial city, the unsullied crystal of its walls and the polish of its golden pavement, when the faces of all the housewives were set Zionward at once.

Now this solemn and earnest view of housekeeping is onerous enough when a poor girl first enters on the care of a moderately furnished house, where the articles are not too expensive to be reasonably renewed as time and use wear them ; but it is infinitely worse when a cataract of splendid furniture is heaped upon her care, — when splendid crystals cut into her conscience, and mirrors reflect her duties, and moth and rust stand ever ready to devour and sully in every room and passage-way.

Sophie was solemnly warned and instructed by all the mothers and aunts, — she was warned of moths, warned of cockroaches, warned of flies, warned of dust ; all the articles of furniture had their covers, made of cold Holland linen, in which they looked like bodies laid out, — even the curtain-tassels had each its little shroud, — and bundles of receipts and of rites and ceremonies necessary for the preservation and purification and care of all these articles were stuffed into the poor girl's head, before guiltless of cares as the feathers that floated above it.

Poor Bill found very soon that his house and furniture were to be kept at such an ideal point of perfection that he needed another house to live in, — for, poor fellow, he found the difference between having a house and a home. It was only a year or two after that my wife and I started our *menage* on very different principles, and Bill would often drop in upon us, wistfully lingering in the cosey arm-chair between my writing-table and my wife's sofa, and saying with a sigh how confoundedly pleasant things looked there, — so pleasant to have a bright, open fire, and geraniums and roses and birds, and all that sort of thing, and to dare to stretch out one's legs and move without thinking what one was going to hit. "Sophie is a good girl!" he would say, "and wants to have everything right, but you see they won't let her. They've loaded her with so many things that have to be kept in lavender, that the poor girl is actually getting thin and losing her health; and then, you see, there's Aunt Zeruah, she mounts guard at our house, and keeps up such strict police-regulations that a fellow can't do a thing. The parlors are splendid, but so lonesome and dismal ! — not a ray of sunshine, in fact not a ray of light, except when a visitor is calling, and then they open a crack. They're afraid of flies, and yet, dear knows, they keep every looking-glass and picture-frame muffled to its throat from March to December. I'd like for curiosity to see what a fly would do in our parlors !"

"Well," said I, "can't you have some little family sitting-room, where you can make yourselves cosey ?"

"Not a bit of it. Sophie and Aunt Zeruah have fixed their throne up in our bedroom, and there they sit all day long, except at calling-hours, and then Sophie dresses herself and comes down. Aunt Zeruah insists upon it that the way is to put the whole house in order, and shut all the blinds, and sit in your bedroom, and then, she says, nothing gets out of place ; and she tells poor Sophie the most hocus-pocus stories about her grandmothers and aunts, who always kept everything in their houses so that they could go and lay their hands on it in the darkest night. I'll bet they could in our house. From end to end it is kept looking as if we had shut it up and gone to Europe, — not a book, not a paper, not a glove, or any trace of a human being, in sight. The piano shut tight, the bookcases shut and locked, the engravings locked up, all the drawers and closets locked. Why, if I want to take a fellow into the library, in the first place it smells like a vault, and I have to unbarricade windows, and unlock and rummage for half an hour before I can get at anything ; and I know Aunt Zeruah is standing tiptoe at the door, ready to whip everything back and lock up again. A fellow can't be social, or take any comfort in showing his books and pictures that way. Then there 's our great, light dining-room, with its sunny south windows, — Aunt Zeruah got us out of that early in April, because she said the flies would speck the frescos and get into the china-closet, and we have been eating in a little dingy den, with a window looking out on a back-alley, ever since ; and Aunt Zeruah says that now the dining-room is always in perfect order, and that it is such a care off Sophie's mind that I ought to be willing to eat down-cellar to the end of the chapter. Now, you see, Chris, my position is a delicate one, because Sophie's folks all agree, that, if there is anything in creation that is ignorant and dreadful and must n't be allowed his way anywhere, it 's 'a man.' Why, you 'd think, to hear Aunt Zeruah talk, that we were all like bulls in a china-shop, ready to toss and tear and rend, if we are not kept down-cellar and chained ; and she worries Sophie, and Sophie's mother comes in and worries, and if I try to get anything done differently,

Sophie cries, and says she don't know what to do, and so I give it up. Now, if I want to ask a few of our set in sociably to dinner, I can't have them where we eat down-cellar, — O, that would never do! Aunt Zeruah and Sophie's mother and the whole family would think the family honor was forever ruined and undone. We must n't ask them, unless we open the dining-room, and have out all the best china, and get the silver home from the bank; and if we do that, Aunt Zeruah does n't sleep for a week beforehand, getting ready for it, and for a week after, getting things put away; and then she tells me, that, in Sophie's delicate state, it really is abominable for me to increase her cares, and so I invite fellows to dine with me at Delmonico's, and then Sophie cries, and Sophie's mother says it does n't look respectable for a family-man to be dining at public places; but, hang it, a fellow wants a home somewhere!"

My wife soothed the chafed spirit, and spake comfortably unto him, and told him that he knew there was the old lounging-chair always ready for him at our fireside. "And you know," she said, "our things are all so plain that we are never tempted to mount any guard over them; our carpets are nothing, and therefore we let the sun fade them, and live on the sunshine and the flowers."

"That 's it," said Bill, bitterly. "Carpets fading!

— that's Aunt Zeruah's monomania. These women think that the great object of houses is to keep out sunshine. What a fool I was, when I gloated over the prospect of our sunny south windows ! Why, man, there are three distinct sets of fortifications against the sunshine in those windows : first, outside blinds ; then, solid, folding, inside shutters ; and, lastly, heavy, thick, lined damask curtains, which loop quite down to the floor. What's the use of my pictures, I desire to know ? They are hung in that room, and it's a regular campaign to get light enough to see what they are."

" But, at all events, you can light them up with gas in the evening."

" In the evening ! Why, do you know my wife never wants to sit there in the evening ? She says she has so much sewing to do that she and Aunt Zeruah must sit up in the bedroom, because it would n't do to bring work into the parlor. Did n't you know that ? Don't you know there must n't be such a thing as a bit of real work ever seen in a parlor ? What if some threads should drop on the carpet ? Aunt Zeruah would have to open all the fortifications next day, and search Jerusalem with candles to find them. No ; in the evening the gas is lighted at half-cock, you know ; and if I turn it up, and bring in my newspapers and spread about me, and pull down some books to read, I can feel the nervousness through the chamber-floor. Aunt Zeruah looks in at eight, and at a quarter past, and at half-past, and at nine, and at ten, to see if I am done, so that she may fold up the papers and put a book on them, and lock up the books in their cases. Nobody ever comes in to spend an evening. They used to try it when we were first married, but I believe the uninhabited appearance of our parlors discouraged them. Everybody has stopped coming now, and Aunt Zeruah says ' it is such a comfort, for now the rooms are always in order. How poor Mrs. Crowfield lives, with her house such a thoroughfare, she is sure she can't see. Sophie never would have strength for it ; but then, to be sure, some folks a'n't as particular as others. Sophie was brought up in a family of *very* particular housekeepers.' "

My wife smiled, with that calm, easy, amused smile that has brightened up her sofa for so many years.

Bill added, bitterly, —

" Of course, I could n't say that I wished the whole set and system of housekeeping women at the — what-'s-his-name ? because Sophie would have cried for a week, and been utterly forlorn and disconsolate. I know it 's not the poor girl's fault ; I try sometimes to reason with her, but you can't reason with the whole of your wife's family, to the third and fourth generation backwards ; but I 'm sure it 's hurting her health,

— wearing her out. Why, you know Sophie used to be the life of our set; and now she really seems eaten up with care from morning to night, there are so many things in the house that something dreadful is happening to all the while, and the servants we get are so clumsy. Why, when I sit with Sophie and Aunt Zeruah, it's nothing but a constant string of complaints about the girls in the kitchen. We keep changing our servants all the time, and they break and destroy so that now we are turned out of the use of all our things. We not only eat in the basement, but all our pretty table-things are put away, and we have all the cracked plates and cracked tumblers and cracked teacups and old buck-handled knives that can be raised out of chaos. I could use these things and be merry, if I did n't know we had better ones; and I can't help wondering whether there is n't some way that our table could be set to look like a gentleman's table; but Aunt Zeruah says that 'it would cost thousands, and what difference does it make as long as nobody sees it but us?' You see, there is no medium in her mind between china and crystal and cracked earthen-ware. Well, I 'm wondering how all these laws of the Medes and Persians are going to work when the children come along. I 'm in hopes the children will soften off the old folks, and make the house more habitable."

Well, children did come, a good many of them, in time. There was Tom, a broad-shouldered, chubby-cheeked, active, hilarious son of mischief, born in the very image of his father ; and there was Charlie, and Jim, and Louisa, and Sophie the second, and Frank, — and a better, brighter, more joy-giving household, as far as temperament and nature were concerned, never existed.

But their whole childhood was a long battle, children *versus* furniture, and furniture always carried the day. The first step of the housekeeping powers was to choose the least agreeable and least available room in the house for the children's nursery, and to fit it up with all the old, cracked, rickety furniture a neighboring auction-shop could afford, and then to keep them in it. Now everybody knows that to bring up children to be upright, true, generous, and religious, needs so much discipline, so much restraint and correction, and so many rules and regulations, that it is all that the parents can carry out, and all the children can bear. There is only a certain amount of the vital force for parents or children to use in this business of education, and one must choose what it shall be used for. The Aunt-Zeruah faction chose to use it for keeping the house and furniture, and the children's education proceeded accordingly. The rules of right and wrong of which they heard most frequently were all of this sort : Naughty children were those who went up the front-stairs, or sat on the best sofa, or fingered any of the books in the library, or got out one of the best teacups, or drank out of the cutglass goblets.

Why did they ever want to do it? If there ever is a forbidden fruit in an Eden, will not our young Adams and Eves risk soul and body to find out how it tastes? Little Tom, the oldest boy, had the courage and enterprise and perseverance of a Captain Parry or Dr. Kane, and he used them all in voyages of discovery to forbidden grounds. He stole Aunt Zeruah's keys, unlocked her cupboards and closets, saw, handled, and tasted everything for himself, and gloried in his sins.

" Don't you know, Tom," said the nurse to him once, " if you are so noisy and rude, you 'll disturb your dear mamma? She 's sick, and she may die, if you 're not careful."

" Will she die ? " says Tom, gravely.

" Why, she *may*."

" Then," said Tom, turning on his heel, — " then I 'll go up the front-stairs."

As soon as ever the little rebel was old enough, he was sent away to boarding-school, and then there was never found a time when it was convenient to have him come home again. He could not come in the spring, for then they were house-cleaning, nor in the autumn, because *then* they were house-cleaning ; and so he spent his vacations at school, unless, by good luck, a companion who was so fortunate as to have a home invited him there. His associations, associates, habits, principles, were as little known to his mother as if she had sent him to China. Aunt Zeruah used to congratulate herself on the rest there was at home, now he was gone, and say she was only living in hopes of the time when Charlie and Jim would be big enough to send away too ; and meanwhile Charlie and Jim, turned out of the charmed circle which should hold growing boys to the father's and mother's side, detesting the dingy, lonely play-room, used to run the city streets, and hang round the railroad depots or docks. Parents may depend upon it, that, if they do not make an attractive resort for their boys, Satan will. There are places enough, kept warm and light and bright and merry, where boys can go whose motheis' parlors are too fine for them to sit in. There are enough to be found to clap them on the back, and tell them stories that their mothers must not hear, and laugh when they compass with their little piping voices the dreadful litanies of sin and shame. In middle life, our poor Sophie, who as a girl was so gay and frolicsome, so full of spirits, had dried and sharpened into a hard-visaged, angular woman, —

careful and troubled about many things, and forgetful that one thing is needful. One of the boys had run away to sea ; 1 believe he has never been heard of. As to Tom, the oldest, he ran a career wild and hard enough for a time, first at school and then in college, and there came a time when he came home, in the full might of six feet two, and almost broke his mother's heart with his assertions of his home rights and privileges. Mothers who throw away the key of their children's hearts and childhood sometimes have a sad retribution. As the children never were considered when they were little and helpless, so they do not consider when they are strong and powerful. Tom spread wide desolation among the household gods, lounging on the sofas, spitting tobacco-juice on the carpets, scattering books and engravings hither and thither, and throwing all the family traditions into wild disorder, as he would never have done, had not all his childish remembrances of them been embittered by the association of restraint and privation. He actually seemed to hate any appearance of luxury or taste or order, — he was a perfect Philistine.

As for my friend Bill, from being the pleasantest and most genial of fellows, he became a morose, misanthropic man. Dr. Franklin has a significant proverb, — " Silks and satins put out the kitchen-fire." Silks and satins — meaning by them the luxuries of housekeeping — often put out not only the parlor-fire, but that more sacred flame, the fire of domestic love. It is the greatest possible misery to a man and to his children to be *homeless ;* and many a man has a splendid house, but no home.

"Papa," said Jenny, "you ought to write and tell what are your ideas of keeping a *home.*"

"Girls, you have only to think how your mother has brought you up."

Nevertheless, I think, being so fortunate a husband, I might reduce my wife's system to an analysis, and my next paper shall be, —

What is a Home, and how to keep it.

III.

WHAT IS A HOME?

IT is among the sibylline secrets which lie mysteriously between you and me, O reader, that these papers, besides their public aspect, have a private one proper to the bosom of mine own particular family.

They are not merely an *ex post facto* protest in regard to that carpet and parlor of celebrated memory, but they are forth-looking towards other homes that may yet arise near us.

For, among my other confidences, you may recollect I stated to you that our Marianne was busy in those interesting cares and details which relate to the preparing and ordering of another dwelling.

Now, when any such matter is going on in a family, I have observed that every feminine instinct is in a state of fluttering vitality, — every woman, old or young, is alive with womanliness to the tips of her fingers ; and it becomes us of the other sex, however consciously respected, to walk softly and put forth our sentiments discreetly and with due reverence for the mysterious powers that reign in the feminine breast.

I had been too well advised to offer one word of direct counsel on a subject where there were such charming voices, so able to convict me of absurdity at every turn. I had merely so arranged my affairs as to put into the hands of my bankers, subject to my wife's order, the very modest marriage-portion which I could place at my girl's disposal ; and Marianne and Jenny, unused to the handling of money, were incessant in their discussions with ever-patient mamma as to what was to be done with it. I say Marianne and Jenny, for, though the case undoubtedly is Marianne's, yet, like everything else in our domestic proceedings, it seems to fall, somehow or other, into Jenny's hands, through the intensity and liveliness of her domesticity of nature. Little Jenny is so bright and wide-awake, and with so many active plans and fancies touching anything in the housekeeping world, that, though the youngest sister, and second party in this affair, a stranger, hearkening to the daily discussions, might listen a half-hour at a time without finding out that it was not Jenny's future establishment that was in question. Marianne is a soft, thoughtful, quiet girl, not given to many words ; and though, when you come fairly at it, you will find, that, like most quiet girls, she has a will

3   D

five times as inflexible as one who talks more, yet
in all family counsels it is Jenny and mamma that
do the discussion, and her own little well-considered
" Yes," or " No," that finally settles each case.

I must add to this family _tableau_ the portrait of
the excellent Bob Stephens, who figured as future
proprietor and householder in these consultations.
So far as the question of financial possibilities is
concerned, it is important to remark that Bob belongs to the class of young Edmunds celebrated
by the poet : —

" Wisdom and worth were all he had."

He is, in fact, an excellent-hearted and clever fellow, with a world of agreeable talents, a good tenor
in a parlor-duet, a good actor at a charade, a lively,
off-hand conversationist, well up in all the current
literature of the day, and what is more, in my eyes,
a well-read lawyer, just admitted to the bar, and with
as fair business prospects as usually fall to the lot of
young aspirants in that profession.

Of course, he and my girl are duly and truly in
love, in all the proper moods and tenses ; but as to
this work they have in hand of being householders,
managing fuel, rent, provision, taxes, gas- and water-
rates, they seem to my older eyes about as sagacious
as a pair of this year's robins. Nevertheless, as the

robins of each year do somehow learn to build nests as well as their ancestors, there is reason to hope as much for each new pair of human creatures. But it is one of the fatalities of our ill-jointed life that houses are usually furnished for future homes by young people in just this state of blissful ignorance of what they are really wanted for, or what is likely to be done with the things in them.

Now, to people of large incomes, with ready wealth for the rectification of mistakes, it does n't much matter how the *menage* is arranged at first ; they will, if they have good sense, soon rid themselves of the little infelicities and absurdities of their first arrangements, and bring their establishment to meet their more instructed tastes.

But to that greater class who have only a modest investment for this first start in domestic life mistakes are far more serious. I have known people go on for years groaning under the weight of domestic possessions they did not want, and pining in vain for others which they did, simply from the fact that all their first purchases were made in this time of blissful ignorance.

I had been a quiet auditor to many animated discussions among the young people as to what they wanted, and were to get, in which the subject of prudence and economy was discussed, with quotations of advice thereon given in serious good-faith by various friends and relations who lived easily on incomes four or five times larger than our own. Who can show the ways of elegant economy more perfectly than people thus at ease in their possessions? From what serene heights do they instruct the inexperienced beginners! Ten thousand a year gives one leisure for reflection, and elegant leisure enables one to view household economies dispassionately; hence the unction with which these gifted daughters of upper-air delight to exhort young neophytes.

"Depend upon it, my dear," Aunt Sophia Easygo had said, "it's always the best economy to get the best things. They cost more in the beginning, but see how they last! These velvet carpets on my floor have been in constant wear for ten years, and look how they wear! I never have an ingrain carpet in my house, — not even on the chambers. Velvet and Brussels cost more to begin with, but then they last. Then I cannot recommend the fashion that is creeping in, of having plate instead of solid silver. Plate wears off, and has to be renewed, which comes to about the same thing in the end as if you bought all solid at first. If I were beginning as Marianne is, I should just set aside a thousand dollars for my silver, and be content with a few plain articles. She should buy all her furniture at Messrs. David and Saul's. People call them dear, but their work will prove cheapest in the end, and there is an air and style about their things that can be told anywhere. Of course, you won't go to any extravagant lengths, — simplicity is a grace of itself."

The waters of the family council were troubled, when Jenny, flaming with enthusiasm, brought home the report of this conversation. When my wife proceeded, with her well-trained business knowledge, to compare the prices of the simplest elegancies recommended by Aunt Easygo with the sum-total to be drawn on, faces lengthened perceptibly.

"How *are* people to go to housekeeping," said Jenny, "if everything costs so much?"

My wife quietly remarked, that we had had great comfort in our own home, — had entertained unnumbered friends, and had only ingrain carpets on our chambers and a three-ply on our parlor, and she doubted if any guest had ever thought of it, — if the rooms had been a shade less pleasant; and as to durability, Aunt Easygo had renewed her carpets oftener than we. Such as ours were, they had worn longer than hers.

"But, mamma, you know everything has gone on since your day. Everybody must at least approach a certain style now-a-days. One can't furnish so far behind other people."

My wife answered in her quiet way, setting forth her doctrine of a plain average to go through the whole establishment, placing parlors, chambers, kitchen, pantries, and the unseen depths of linen-closets in harmonious relations of just proportion, and showed by calm estimates how far the sum given could go towards this result. *There* the limits were inexorable. There is nothing so damping to the ardor of youthful economies as the hard, positive logic of figures. It is so delightful to think in some airy way that the things we *like* best are the cheapest, and that a sort of rigorous duty compels us to get them at any sacrifice. There is no remedy for this illusion but to show by the multiplication and addition tables what things are and are not possible. My wife's figures met Aunt Easygo's assertions, and there was a lull among the high contracting parties for a season ; nevertheless, I could see Jenny was secretly uneasy. I began to hear of journeys made to far places, here and there, where expensive articles of luxury were selling at reduced prices. Now a gilded mirror was discussed, and now a velvet carpet which chance had brought down temptingly near the sphere of financial possibility. I thought of our parlor, and prayed the good fairies to avert the advent of ill-assorted articles.

"Pray keep common sense uppermost in the girls' heads, if you can," said I to Mrs. Crowfield, "and

don't let the poor little puss spend her money for
what she won't care a button about by and by."

"I shall try," she said ; "but you know Marianne
is inexperienced, and Jenny is so ardent and active,
and so confident, too. Then they both, I think, have
the impression that we are a little behind the age.
To say the truth, my dear, I think your papers afford
a good opportunity of dropping a thought now and
then in their minds. Jenny was asking last night
when you were going to write your next paper. The
girl has a bright, active mind, and thinks of what she
hears."

So flattered, by the best of flatterers, I sat down
to write on my theme ; and that evening, at fire-light
time, I read to my little senate as follows : —

WHAT IS A HOME, AND HOW TO KEEP IT.

I HAVE shown that a dwelling, rented or owned by
a man, in which his own wife keeps house, is not
always, or of course, a home. What is it, then, that
makes a home? All men and women have the indefinite knowledge of what they want and long for
when that word is spoken. "Home!" sighs the disconsolate bachelor, tired of boarding-house fare and
buttonless shirts. "Home!" says the wanderer in
foreign lands, and thinks of mother's love, of wife

and sister and child. Nay, the word has in it a higher
meaning, hallowed by religion ; and when the Christian would express the highest of his hopes for a
better life, he speaks of his *home* beyond the grave.
The word home has in it the elements of love, rest,
permanency, and liberty ; but besides these it has in
it the idea of an education by which all that is purest
within us is developed into nobler forms, fit for a
higher life. The little child by the home-fireside was
taken on the Master's knee when he would explain to
his disciples the mysteries of the kingdom.

Of so great dignity and worth is this holy and
sacred thing, that the power to create a HOME ought
to be ranked above all creative faculties. The sculp-
tor who brings out the breathing statue from cold
marble, the painter who warms the canvas into a
deathless glow of beauty, the architect who built ca-
thedrals and hung the world-like dome of St. Peter's
in mid-air, is not to be compared, in sanctity and
worthiness, to the humblest artist, who, out of the
poor materials afforded by this shifting, changing,
selfish world, creates the secure Eden of a *home.*

A true home should be called the noblest work of
art possible to human creatures, inasmuch as it is the
very image chosen to represent the last and highest
rest of the soul, the consummation of man's blessed-
ness.

Not without reason does the oldest Christian church require of those entering on marriage the most solemn review of all the past life, the confession and repentance of every sin of thought, word, and deed, and the reception of the holy sacrament; for thus the man and woman who approach the august duty of creating a home are reminded of the sanctity and beauty of what they undertake.

In this art of home-making I have set down in my mind certain first principles, like the axioms of Euclid, and the first is, —

No home is possible without love.

All business marriages and marriages of convenience, all mere culinary marriages and marriages of mere animal passion, make the creation of a true home impossible in the outset. Love is the jewelled foundation of this New Jerusalem descending from God out of heaven, and takes as many bright forms as the amethyst, topaz, and sapphire of that mysterious vision. In this range of creative art all things are possible to him that loveth, but without love nothing is possible.

We hear of most convenient marriages in foreign lands, which may better be described as commercial partnerships. The money on each side is counted; there is enough between the parties to carry on the firm, each having the appropriate sum allotted to

3 *

each. No love is pretended, but there is great politeness. All is so legally and thoroughly arranged, that there seems to be nothing left for future quarrels to fasten on. Monsieur and Madame have each their apartments, their carriages, their servants, their income, their friends, their pursuits, — understand the solemn vows of marriage to mean simply that they are to treat each other with urbanity in those few situations where the path of life must necessarily bring them together.

We are sorry that such an idea of marriage should be gaining foothold in America. It has its root in an ignoble view of life, — an utter and pagan darkness as to all that man and woman are called to do in that highest relation where they act as one. It is a mean and low contrivance on both sides, by which all the grand work of home-building, all the noble pains and heroic toils of home-education, — that education where the parents learn more than they teach, — shall be (let us use the expressive Yankee idiom) *shirked*.

It is a curious fact that in those countries where this system of marriages is the general rule there is no word corresponding to our English word *home*. In many polite languages of Europe it would be impossible neatly to translate the sentiment with which we began this essay, that a man's *house* is not always his *home*.

Let any one try to render the song, "Sweet Home," into French, and one finds how Anglo-Saxon is the very genius of the word. The structure of life, in all its relations, in countries where marriages are matter of arrangement, and not of love, excludes the idea of home.

How does life run in such countries? The girl is recalled from her convent or boarding-school, and told that her father has found a husband for her. No objection on her part is contemplated or provided for; none generally occurs, for the child is only too happy to obtain the fine clothes and the liberty which she has been taught come only with marriage. Be the man handsome or homely, interesting or stupid, still he brings these.

How intolerable such a marriage! we say, with the close intimacies of Anglo-Saxon life in our minds. They are not intolerable, because they are provided for by arrangements which make it possible for each to go his or her several way, seeing very little of the other. The son or daughter, which in due time makes its appearance in this *menage*, is sent out to nurse in infancy, sent to boarding-school in youth, and in maturity portioned and married, to repeat the same process for another generation. Meanwhile, father and mother keep a quiet establishment, and pursue their several pleasures. Such is the system.

Houses built for this kind of life become mere sets
of reception-rooms, such as are the greater proportion
of apartments to let in Paris, where a hearty English
or American family, with their children about them,
could scarcely find room to establish themselves.
Individual character, it is true, does something to
modify this programme. There are charming homes
in France and Italy, where warm and noble natures,
thrown together, perhaps, by accident, or mated by
wise paternal choice, infuse warmth into the coldness
of the system under which they live. There are in
all states of society some of such domesticity of
nature that they will create a home around themselves under any circumstances, however barren. Besides, so kindly is human nature, that Love uninvited
before marriage, often becomes a guest after, and with
Love always comes a home.

My next axiom is, —

There can be no true home without liberty.

The very idea of home is of a retreat where we
shall be free to act out personal and individual tastes
and peculiarities, as we cannot do before the wide
world. We are to have our meals at what hour we
will, served in what style suits us. Our hours of
going and coming are to be as we please. Our favorite haunts are to be here or there, our pictures and
books so disposed as seems to us good, and our

whole arrangements the expression, so far as our
means can compass it, of our own personal ideas of
what is pleasant and desirable in life. This element
of liberty, if we think of it, is the chief charm of
home. "Here I can do as I please," is the thought
with which the tempest-tossed earth-pilgrim blesses
himself or herself, turning inward from the crowded
ways of the world. This thought blesses the man of
business, as he turns from his day's care, and crosses
the sacred threshold. It is as restful to him as the
slippers and gown and easy-chair by the fireside.
Everybody understands him here. Everybody is well
content that he should take his ease in his own way.
Such is the case in the *ideal* home. That such is not
always the case in the real home comes often from
the mistakes in the house-furnishing. Much house-
furnishing is *too fine* for liberty.

In America there is no such thing as rank and
station which impose a sort of prescriptive style on
people of certain income. The consequence is that
all sorts of furniture and belongings, which in the Old
World have a recognized relation to certain possibilities of income, and which require certain other accessories to make them in good keeping, are thrown in
the way of all sorts of people.

Young people who cannot expect by any reasonable
possibility to keep more than two or three servants, if

they happen to have the means in the outset, furnish a house with just such articles as in England would suit an establishment of sixteen. We have seen houses in England having two or three house-maids, and tables served by a butler and two waiters, where the furniture, carpets, china, crystal, and silver were in one and the same style with some establishments in America where the family was hard pressed to keep three Irish servants.

This want of servants is the one thing that must modify everything in American life; it is, and will long continue to be, a leading feature in the life of a country so rich in openings for man and woman that domestic service can be only the stepping-stone to something higher. Nevertheless, we Americans are great travellers ; we are sensitive, appreciative, fond of novelty, apt to receive and incorporate into our own life what seems fair and graceful in that of other people. Our women's wardrobes are made elaborate with the thousand elegancies of French toilet,—our houses filled with a thousand knick-knacks of which our plain ancestors never dreamed. Cleopatra did not set sail on the Nile in more state and beauty than that in which our young American bride is often ushered into her new home. Her wardrobe all gossamer lace and quaint frill and crimp and embroidery, her house a museum of elegant and costly gewgaws ; and amid the whole collection of elegancies and fragilities, she, perhaps, the frailest.

Then comes the tug of war. The young wife becomes a mother, and while she is retired to her chamber, blundering Biddy rusts the elegant knives, or takes off the ivory handles by soaking in hot water, —the silver is washed in greasy soap-suds, and refreshed now and then with a thump, which cocks the nose of the teapot awry, or makes the handle assume an air of drunken defiance. The fragile China is chipped here and there around its edges with those minute gaps so vexatious to a woman's soul; the handles fly hither and thither in the wild confusion of Biddy's washing-day hurry, when cook wants her to help hang out the clothes. Meanwhile, Bridget sweeps the parlor with a hard broom, and shakes out showers of ashes from the grate, forgetting to cover the damask lounges, and they directly look as rusty and time-worn as if they had come from an auction-store; and all together unite in making such havoc of the delicate ruffles and laces of the bridal outfit and baby-*layette*, that, when the poor young wife comes out of her chamber after her nurse has left her, and, weakened and embarrassed with the demands of the new-comer, begins to look once more into the affairs of her little world, she is ready to sink with vexation and discouragement. Poor little princess!

Her clothes are made as princesses wear them, her baby's clothes like a young duke's, her house furnished like a lord's, and only Bridget and Biddy and Polly to do the work of cook, scullery-maid, butler, footman, laundress, nursery-maid, house-maid, and lady's maid. Such is the array that in the Old Country would be deemed necessary to take care of an establishment got up like hers. Everything in it is *too fine*, — not too fine to be pretty, not in bad taste in itself, but too fine for the situation, too fine for comfort or liberty.

What ensues in a house so furnished ? Too often ceaseless fretting of the nerves, in the wife's despairing, conscientious efforts to keep things as they should be. There is no freedom in a house where things are too expensive and choice to be freely handled and easily replaced. Life becomes a series of petty embarrassments and restrictions, something is always going wrong, and the man finds his fireside oppressive, — the various articles of his parlor and table seem like so many temper-traps and spring-guns, menacing explosion and disaster.

There may be, indeed, the most perfect home-feeling, the utmost coseyness and restfulness, in apartments crusted with gilding, carpeted with velvet, and upholstered with satin. I have seen such, where the home-like look and air of free use was as genuine as in a Western log-cabin ; but this was in a range of princely income that made all these things as easy to be obtained or replaced as the most ordinary of our domestic furniture. But so long as articles must be shrouded from use, or used with fear and trembling, because their cost is above the general level of our means, we had better be without them, even though the most lucky of accidents may put their possession in our power.

But it is not merely by the effort to maintain too much elegance that the sense of home-liberty is banished from a house. It is sometimes expelled in another way, with all painstaking and conscientious strictness, by the worthiest and best of human beings, the blessed followers of Saint Martha. Have we not known them, the dear, worthy creatures, up before daylight, causing most scrupulous lustrations of every pane of glass and inch of paint in our parlors, in consequence whereof every shutter and blind must be kept closed for days to come, lest the flies should speck the freshly washed windows and wainscoting ? Dear shade of Aunt Mehitabel, forgive our boldness ? Have we not been driven for days, in our youth, to read our newspaper in the front veranda, in the kitchen, out in the barn, — anywhere, in fact, where sunshine could be found, because there was not a room in the house that was not cleaned, shut up,

E

and darkened? Have we not shivered with cold, all the glowering, gloomy month of May, because the august front-parlor having undergone the spring cleaning, the andirons were snugly tied up in the tissue-paper, and an elegant frill of the same material was trembling before the mouth of the once glowing fireplace? Even so, dear soul, full of loving-kindness and hospitality as thou wast, yet ever making our house seem like a tomb! And with what patience wouldst thou sit sewing by a crack in the shutters, an inch wide, rejoicing in thy immaculate paint and clear glass! But was there ever a thing of thy spotless and unsullied belongings which a boy might use? How I trembled to touch thy scoured tins, that hung in appalling brightness! with what awe I asked for a basket to pick strawberries! and where in the house could I find a place to eat a piece of gingerbread? How like a ruffian, a Tartar, a pirate, I always felt, when I entered thy domains! and how, from day to day, I wondered at the immeasurable depths of depravity which were always leading me to upset something, or break or tear or derange something, in thy exquisitely kept premises! Somehow, the impression was burned with overpowering force into my mind, that houses and furniture, scrubbed floors, white curtains, bright tins and brasses were the great, awful, permanent facts of existence, — and that men and women, and particularly children, were the meddlesome intruders upon this divine order, every trace of whose inter-meddling must be scrubbed out and obliterated in the quickest way possible. It seemed evident to me that houses would be far more perfect, if no-body lived in them at all; but that, as men had really and absurdly taken to living in them, they must live as little as possible. My only idea of a house was a place full of traps and pitfalls for boys, a deadly temptation to sins which beset one every moment; and when I read about a sailor's free life on the ocean, I felt an untold longing to go forth and be free in like manner.

But a truce to these fancies, and back again to our essay.

If liberty in a house is a comfort to a husband, it is a necessity to children. When we say liberty, we do not mean license. We do not mean that Master Johnny be allowed to handle elegant volumes with bread-and-butter fingers, or that little Miss be suf-fered to drum on the piano, or practise line-drawing with a pin on varnished furniture. Still it is essen-tial that the family-parlors be not too fine for the family to sit in, — too fine for the ordinary accidents, haps and mishaps, of reasonably well-trained children. The elegance of the parlor where papa and mamma sit and receive their friends should wear an inviting, not a hostile and bristling, aspect to little people. Its beauty and its order gradually form in the little mind a love of beauty and order, and the insensible carefulness of regard.

Nothing is worse for a child than to shut him up in a room which he understands is his, *because* he is disorderly, — where he is expected, of course, to maintain and keep disorder. We have sometimes pitied the poor little victims who show their faces longingly at the doors of elegant parlors, and are forthwith collared by the domestic police and consigned to some attic-apartment, called a play-room, where chaos continually reigns. It is a mistake to suppose, because children derange a well-furnished apartment, that they like confusion. Order and beauty are always pleasant to them as to grown people, and disorder and deface-ment are painful ; but they know neither how to create the one nor to prevent the other, — their little lives are a series of experiments, often making disorder by aiming at some new form of order. Yet, for all this, I am not one of those who feel that in a family everything should bend to the sway of these little people. They are the worst of tyrants in such houses, — still, where children are, though the fact must not appear to them, *nothing must be done without a wise thought of them.*

Here, as in all high art, the old motto is in force, "*Ars est celare artem.*" Children who are taught too plainly by every anxious look and word of their parents, by every family arrangement, by the impressment of every chance guest into the service, that their parents consider their education as the one important matter in creation, are apt to grow up fantastical, artificial, and hopelessly self-conscious. The stars cannot stop in their courses, even for our personal improvement, and the sooner children learn this, the better. The great art is to organize a home which shall move on with a strong, wide, generous movement, where the little people shall act themselves out as freely and impulsively as can consist with the comfort of the whole, and where the anxious watching and planning for them shall be kept as secret from them as possible.

It is well that one of the sunniest and airiest rooms in the house be the children's nursery. It is good philosophy, too, to furnish it attractively, even if the sum expended lower the standard of parlor-luxuries. It is well that the children's chamber, which is to act constantly on their impressible natures for years, should command a better prospect, a sunnier aspect, than one which serves for a day's occupancy of the transient guest. It is well that journeys should be made or put off in view of the interests of the chil-

dren, — that guests should be invited with a view to
their improvement, — that some intimacies should be
chosen and some rejected on their account. But it
is *not* well that all this should, from infancy, be daily
talked out before the child, and he grow up in egotism
from moving in a sphere where everything from first
to last is calculated and arranged with reference to
himself. A little appearance of wholesome neglect
combined with real care and never-ceasing watchfulness has often seemed to do wonders in this work
of setting human beings on their own feet for the
life-journey.

Education is the highest object of home, but education in the widest sense, — education of the parents
no less than of the children. In a true home the
man and the woman receive, through their cares,
their watchings, their hospitality, their charity, the
last and highest finish that earth can put upon them.
From that they must pass upward, for earth can teach
them no more.

The home-education is incomplete, unless it include
the idea of hospitality and charity. Hospitality is a
Biblical and apostolic virtue, and not so often recommended in Holy Writ without reason. Hospitality
is much neglected in America for the very reasons
touched upon above. We have received our ideas
of propriety and elegance of living from old coun-

tries, where labor is cheap, where domestic service is a well-understood, permanent occupation, adopted cheerfully for life, and where of course there is such a subdivision of labor as insures great thoroughness in all its branches. We are ashamed or afraid to conform honestly and hardily to a state of things purely American. We have not yet accomplished what our friend the Doctor calls " our weaning," and learned that dinners with circuitous courses and divers other Continental and English refinements, well enough in their way, cannot be accomplished in families with two or three untrained servants, without an expense of care and anxiety which makes them heart-withering· to the delicate wife, and too severe a trial to occur often. America is the land of subdivided fortunes, of a general average of wealth and comfort, and there ought to be, therefore, an understanding in the social basis far more simple than ·in the Old World.

Many families of small fortunes know this, — they are quietly living so, — but they have not the steadiness to share their daily average living with a friend, a traveller, or guest, just as the Arab shares his tent and the Indian his bowl of succotash. They cannot have company, they say. Why? Because it is such a fuss to get out the best things, and then to put them back again. But why get out the best things?

Why not give your friend, what he would like a thousand times better, a bit of your average home-life, a seat at any time at your board, a seat at your fire? If he sees that there is a handle off your teacup, and that there is a crack across one of your plates, he only thinks, with a sigh of relief, "Well, mine are n't the only things that meet with accidents," and he feels nearer to you ever after; he will let you come to his table and see the cracks in his teacups, and you will condole with each other on the transient nature of earthly possessions. If it become apparent in these entirely undressed rehearsals that your children are sometimes disorderly, and that your cook sometimes overdoes the meat, and that your second girl sometimes is awkward in waiting, or has forgotten a table propriety, your friend only feels, "Ah, well, other people have trials as well as I," and he thinks, if you come to see him, he shall feel easy with you.

"*Having company*" is an expense that may always be felt; but easy daily hospitality, the plate always on your table for a friend, is an expense that appears on no account-book, and a pleasure that is daily and constant.

Under this head of hospitality, let us suppose a case. A traveller comes from England; he comes in good faith and good feeling to see how Americans live. He merely wants to penetrate into the interior of domestic life, to see. what there is genuinely and peculiarly American about it. Now here is Smilax, who is living, in a small, neat way, on his salary from the daily press. He remembers hospitalities received from our traveller in England, and wants to return them. He remembers, too, with dismay, a well-kept establishment, the well-served table, the punctilious, orderly servants. Smilax keeps two, a cook and chambermaid, who divide the functions of his establishment between them. What shall he do? Let him say, in a fair, manly way, "My dear fellow, I'm delighted to see you. I live in a small way, but I'll do my best for you, and Mrs. Smilax will be delighted. Come and dine with us, so and so, and we'll bring in one or two friends." So the man comes, and Mrs. Smilax serves up such a dinner as lies within the limits of her knowledge and the capacities of her servants. All plain, good of its kind, unpretending, without an attempt to do anything English or French, — to do anything more than if she were furnishing a gala-dinner for her father or returned brother. Show him your house freely, just as it is, talk to him freely of it, just as he in England showed you his larger house and talked to you of his finer things. If the man is a true man, he will thank you for such unpretending, sincere welcome; if he is a man of straw, then he is not worth wasting Mrs. Smilax's health and spirits for, in unavailing efforts to get up a foreign dinner-party.

A man who has any heart in him values a genuine, little bit of home more than anything else you can give him. He can get French cooking at a restaurant; he can buy expensive wines at first-class hotels, if he wants them; but the traveller, though ever so rich and ever so well-served at home, is, after all, nothing but a man as you are, and he is craving something that does n't seem like an hotel, — some bit of real, genuine heart-life. Perhaps he would like better than anything to show you the last photograph of his wife, or to read to you the great, round-hand letter of his ten-year-old which he has got to-day. He is ready to cry when he thinks of it. In this mood he goes to see you, hoping for something like home, and you first receive him in a parlor opened only on state occasions, and that has been circumstantially and exactly furnished, as the upholsterer assures you, as every other parlor of the kind in the city is furnished. You treat him to a dinner got up for the occasion, with hired waiters, — a dinner which it has taken Mrs. Smilax a week to prepare for, and will take her a week to recover from, — for which the baby has been snubbed and turned off, to his loud indignation, and your young four-year-old sent to his aunts. Your traveller eats your dinner, and finds it inferior, as a

work of art, to other dinners,—a poor imitation. He
goes away and criticises ; you hear of it, and resolve
never to invite a foreigner again. But if you had
given him a little of your heart, a little home-warmth
and feeling, — if you had shown him your baby, and
let him romp with your four-year-old, and eat a genuine dinner with you, — would he have been false to
that? Not so likely. He wanted something real and
human, — you gave him a bad dress-rehearsal, and
dress-rehearsals always provoke criticism.

Besides hospitality, there is, in a true home, a mission of charity., It is a just law which regulates the
possession of great or beautiful works of art in the
Old World, that they shall in some sense be considered the property of all who can appreciate. Fine
grounds have hours when the public may be admitted,
— pictures and statues may be shown to visitors ; and
this is a noble charity. In the same manner the fortunate individuals who have achieved the greatest of
all human works of art should employ it as a sacred
charity. How many, morally wearied, wandering, dis-
abled, are healed and comforted by the warmth of a
true home! When a mother has sent her son to the
temptations of a distant city, what news is so glad to
her heart as that he has found some quiet family
where he visits often and is made to feel AT HOME?
How many young men have good women saved from

temptation and shipwreck by drawing them often to
the sheltered corner by the fireside ! The poor artist,
— the wandering genius who has lost his way in this
world, and stumbles like a child among hard realities,
— the many men and women who, while they have
houses, have no homes, — see from afar, in their distant, bleak life-journey, the light of a true home-fire,
and, if made welcome there, warm their stiffened
limbs, and go forth stronger to their pilgrimage. Let
those who have accomplished this beautiful and perfect work of divine art be liberal of its influence. Let
them not seek to bolt the doors and draw the curtains ; for they know not, and will never know till the
future life, of the good they may do by the ministration of this great charity of home.

We have heard much lately of the restricted sphere
of woman. We have been told how many spirits
among women are of a wider, stronger, more heroic
mould than befits the mere routine of housekeeping.
It may be true that there are many women far too
great, too wise, too high, for mere housekeeping.
But where is the woman in any way too great or too
high, or too wise, to spend herself in creating a
home? What can any woman make diviner, higher,
better? From such homes go forth all heroisms, all
inspirations, all great deeds. Such mothers and such
homes have made the heroes and martyrs, faithful

unto death, who have given their precious lives to us during these three years of our agony !

Homes are the work of art peculiar to the genius of woman. Man *helps* in this work, but woman leads ; the hive is always in confusion without the *queen*-bee. But what a woman must she be who does this work perfectly ! She comprehends all, she balances and arranges all ; all different tastes and temperaments find in her their rest, and she can unite at one hearthstone the most discordant elements. In her is order, yet an order ever veiled and concealed by indulgence. None are checked, reproved, abridged of privileges by her love of system ; for she knows that order was made for the family, and not the family for order. Quietly she takes on herself what all others refuse or overlook. What the unwary disarrange she silently rectifies. Everybody in her sphere breathes easy, feels free ; and the driest twig begins in her sunshine to put out buds and blossoms. So quiet are her operations and movements, that none sees that it is she who holds all things in harmony ; only, alas, when she is gone, how many things suddenly appear disordered, inharmonious, neglected ! All these threads have been smilingly held in her weak hand. Alas, if that is no longer there !

Can any woman be such a housekeeper without inspiration ? No. In the words of the old church-

service, "Her soul must ever have affiance in God."
The New Jerusalem of a perfect home cometh down
from God out of heaven.   But to make such a home
is ambition high and worthy enough for *any* woman,
be she what she may.

One thing more.   Right on the threshold of all perfection lies *the cross* to be taken up.   No one can go
over or around that cross in science or in art.   Without labor and self-denial neither Raphael nor Michel
Angelo nor Newton was made perfect.   Nor can man
or woman create a true home who is not willing in the
outset to embrace life heroically, to encounter labor
and sacrifice.   Only to such shall this divinest power
be given to create on earth that which is the nearest
image of heaven.

IV.

THE ECONOMY OF THE BEAUTIFUL.

TALKING to you in this way once a month, O
my confidential reader, there seems to be danger, as in all intervals of friendship, that we shall not
readily be able to take up our strain of conversation
just where we left off. Suffer me, therefore, to remind
you that the month past left us seated at the fireside,
just as we had finished reading of what a home was,
and how to make one.

The fire had burned low, and great, solid hickory
coals were winking dreamily at us from out their fluffy
coats of white ashes, — just as if some household
sprite there were opening now one eye and then the
other, and looking in a sleepy, comfortable way at us.

The close of my piece, about the good house-
mother, had seemed to tell on my little audience.
Marianne had nestled close to her mother, and laid
her head on her knee ; and though Jenny sat up
straight as a pin, yet her ever-busy knitting was
dropped in her lap, and I saw the glint of a tear in
her quick, sparkling eye, — yes, actually a little bright

bead fell upon her. work ; whereupon she started up actively, and declared that the fire wanted just one more stick to make a blaze before bedtime ; and then there was such a raking among the coals, such an adjusting of the andirons, such vigorous arrangement of the wood, and such a brisk whisking of the hearth-brush, that it was evident Jenny had something on her mind.

When all was done, she sat down again and looked straight into the blaze, which went dancing and crackling up, casting glances and flecks of light on our pictures and books, and making all the old, familiar furniture seem full of life and motion.

" I think that 's a good piece," she said, decisively. " I think those are things that should be thought about."

Now Jenny was the youngest of our flock, and therefore, in a certain way, regarded by my wife and me as perennially " the baby " ; and these little, old-fashioned, decisive ways of announcing her opinions seemed so much a part of her nature, so peculiarly " Jennyish," as I used to say, that my wife and I only exchanged amused glances over her head, when they occurred.

In a general way, Jenny; standing in the full orb of her feminine instincts like Diana in the moon, rather looked down on all masculine views of women's matters as "*tolerabiles ineptiæ*" ; but towards her papa she had gracious turns of being patronizing to the last degree ; and one of these turns was evidently at its flood-tide, as she proceeded to say, —

"*I* think papa is right, — that keeping house and having a home, and all that, is a very serious thing, and that people go into it with very little thought about it. I really think those things papa has been saying there ought to be thought about."

"Papa," said Marianne, "I wish you would tell me exactly how *you* would spend that money you gave me for house-furnishing. I should like just your views."

"Precisely," said Jenny, with eagerness ; "because it is just as papa says, — a sensible man, who has thought, and had experience, can't help having some ideas, even about women's affairs, that are worth attending to. I think so, decidedly."

I acknowledged the compliment for my sex and myself with my best bow.

"But then, papa," said Marianne, "I can't help feeling sorry that one can't live in such a way as to have beautiful things around one. I 'm sorry they must cost so much, and take so much care, for I am made so that I really want them. I do so like to see pretty things ! I do like rich carpets and elegant carved furniture, and fine china and cut-glass and silver. I can't bear mean, common-looking rooms. I should so like to have my house look beautiful!"

"Your house ought not to look mean and common, — your house ought to look beautiful," I replied. "It would be a sin and a shame to have it otherwise. No house ought to be fitted up for a future home without a strong and a leading reference to beauty in all its arrangements. If I were a Greek, I should say that the first household libation should be made to beauty; but, being an old-fashioned Christian, I would say that he who prepares a home with no eye to beauty neglects the example of the great Father who has filled our earth-home with such elaborate ornament."

"But then, papa, there's the money!" said Jenny, shaking her little head wisely. "You men don't think of that. You want us girls, for instance, to be patterns of economy, but we must always be wearing fresh, nice things; you abhor soiled gloves and worn shoes: and yet how is all this to be done without money? And it's just so in housekeeping. You sit in your arm-chairs and conjure up visions of all sorts of impossible things to be done; but when mamma there takes out that little account-book, and figures away on the cost of things, where do the visions go?"

"You are mistaken, my little dear, and you talk just like a woman," — (this was *my* only way of revenging myself,) — "that is to say, you jump to conclusions, without sufficient knowledge. I maintain that in house-furnishing, as well as woman-furnishing, there 's nothing so economical as beauty."

"There 's one of papa's paradoxes !" said Jenny.

"Yes," said I, "that is my thesis, which I shall nail up over the mantel-piece there, as Luther nailed his to the church-door. It is time to rake up the fire now ; but to-morrow night I will give you a paper on the Economy of the Beautiful."

*   *   *   *   *

"Come, now we are to have papa's paradox," said Jenny, as soon as the tea-things had been carried out.

Entre nous, I must tell you that insensibly we had fallen into the habit of taking our tea by my study-fire. Tea, you know, is a mere nothing in itself, its only merit being its social and poetic associations, its warmth and fragrance, — and the more socially and informally it can be dispensed, the more in keeping with its airy and cheerful nature.

Our circle was enlightened this evening by the cheery visage of Bob Stephens, seated, as of right, close to Marianne's work-basket.

"You see, Bob," said Jenny, "papa has undertaken to prove that the most beautiful things are always the cheapest."

"I 'm glad to hear that," said Bob, — "for there 's a carved antique bookcase and study-table that I have my eye on, and if this can in any way be made to appear —"

"O, it won't be made to appear," said Jenny, settling herself at her knitting, "only in some transcendental, poetic sense, such as papa can always make out. Papa is more than half a poet, and his truths turn out to be figures of rhetoric, when one comes to apply them to matters of fact."

"Now, Miss Jenny, please remember my subject and thesis," I replied, — "that in house-furnishing there is nothing so economical as beauty; and I will make it good against all comers, not by figures of rhetoric, but by figures of arithmetic. I am going to be very matter-of-fact and commonplace in my details, and keep ever in view the addition-table. I will instance a case which has occurred under my own observation."

The Economy of the Beautiful.

Two of the houses lately built on the new land in Boston were bought by two friends, Philip and John. Philip had plenty of money, and paid the cash down for his house, without feeling the slightest vacancy in his pocket. John, who was an active, rising young man, just entering on a flourishing business, had expended all his moderate savings for years in the purchase of his dwelling, and still had a mortgage remaining, which he hoped to clear off by his future successes. Philip begins the work of furnishing as people do with whom money is abundant, and who have simply to go from shop to shop and order all that suits their fancy and is considered 'the thing' in good society. John begins to furnish with very little money. He has a wife and two little ones, and he wisely deems that to insure to them a well-built house, in an open, airy situation, with conveniences for warming, bathing, and healthy living, is a wise beginning in life ; but it leaves him little or nothing beyond.

Behold, then, Philip and his wife, well pleased, going the rounds of shops and stores in fitting up their new dwelling, and let us follow step by step. To begin with the wall-paper. Imagine a front and back parlor, with folding-doors, with two south windows on the front, and two looking on a back court, after the general manner of city houses. We will suppose they require about thirty rolls of wall-paper. Philip buys the heaviest French velvet, with gildings and traceries, at four dollars a roll. This, by the time it has been put on, with gold mouldings, according to the most established taste of the best paper-hangers, will bring the wall-paper of the two rooms to a figure something like two hundred dollars. Now they proceed to the carpet-stores, and there are thrown at

their feet by obsequious clerks velvets and Axmin-
sters, with flowery convolutions and medallion-centres,
as if the flower-gardens of the tropics were whirling
in waltzes, with graceful lines of arabesque, — roses,
callas, lilies, knotted, wreathed, twined, with blue and
crimson and golden ribbons, dazzling marvels of color
and tracery. There is no restraint in price, — four or
six dollars a yard, it is all the same to them, — and
soon a magic flower-garden blooms on the floors, at a
cost of five hundred dollars. A pair of elegant rugs,
at fifty dollars apiece, complete the inventory, and
bring our rooms to the mark of eight hundred dollars
for papering and carpeting alone. Now come the
great mantel-mirrors for four hundred more, and our
rooms progress. Then comes the upholsterer, and
measures our four windows, that he may skilfully bar-
ricade them from air and sunshine. The fortifications
against heaven, thus prepared, cost, in the shape of
damask, cord, tassels, shades, laces, and cornices,
about two hundred dollars per window. To be sure,
they make the rooms close and sombre as the grave ;
but they are of the most splendid stuffs ; and if the
sun would only reflect, he would see, himself, how
foolish it was for him to try to force himself into a
window guarded by his betters. If there is anything
cheap and plebeian, it is sunshine and fresh air ! Behold us, then, with our two rooms papered, carpeted,

and curtained for two thousand dollars ; and now are to be put in them sofas, lounges, étagères, centre-tables, screens, chairs of every pattern and device, for which it is but moderate to allow a thousand more. We have now two parlors furnished at an outlay of three thousand dollars, without a single picture, a single article of statuary, a single object of Art of any kind, and without any light to see them by, if they were there. We must say for our Boston upholsterers and furniture-makers that such good taste generally reigns in their establishments that rooms furnished at hap-hazard from them cannot fail of a certain air of good taste, so far as the individual things are concerned. But the different articles we have supposed, having been ordered without reference to one another or the rooms, have, when brought together, no unity of effect, and the general result is scattering and confused. If asked how Philip's parlors look, your reply is, " O, the usual way of such parlors, — everything that such people usually get, — medallion-carpets, carved furniture, great mirrors, bronze mantel-ornaments, and so on." The only impression a stranger receives, while waiting in the dim twilight of these rooms, is that their owner is rich, and able to get good, handsome things, such as all other rich people get.

Now our friend John, as often happens in America,

is moving in the same social circle with Philip, visiting the same people, — his house is the twin of the one Philip has been furnishing, and how shall he, with a few hundred dollars, make his rooms even presentable beside those which Philip has fitted up elegantly at three thousand?

Now for the economy of beauty. Our friend must make his prayer to the Graces, — for, if they cannot save him, nobody can. One thing John has to begin with, that rare gift to man, a wife with the magic cestus of Venus, — not around her waist, but, if such a thing could be, in her finger-ends. All that she touches falls at once into harmony and proportion. Her eye for color and form is intuitive : let her arrange a garret, with nothing but boxes, barrels, and cast-off furniture in it, and ten to one she makes it seem the most attractive place in the house. It is a veritable " gift of good faërie," this tact of beautifying and arranging, that some women have, — and, on the present occasion, it has a real, material value, that can be estimated in dollars and cents. Come with us and you can see the pair taking their survey of the yet unfurnished parlors, as busy and happy as a couple of bluebirds picking up the first sticks and straws for their nest.

" There are two sunny windows to begin with," says the good fairy, with an appreciative glance. " That insures flowers all winter."

"Yes," says John ; "I never would look at a house without a good sunny exposure. Sunshine is the best ornament of a house, and worth an extra thousand a year."

"Now for our wall-paper," says she. "Have you looked at wall-papers, John ? "

"Yes ; we shall get very pretty ones for thirty-seven cents a roll ; all you want of a paper, you know, is to make a ground-tint to throw out your pictures and other matters, and to reflect a pleasant tone of light."

"Well, John, you know Uncle James says that a stone-color is the best, — but I can't bear those cold blue grays."

"Nor I," says John. "If we must have gray, let it at least be a gray suffused with gold or rose-color, such as you see at evening in the clouds."

"So I think," responds she ; "but, better, I should like a paper with a tone of buff, — something that produces warm yellowish reflections, and will almost make you think the sun is shining in cold gray weather ; and then there is nothing that lights up so cheerfully in the evening. In short, John, I think the color of a *zafferano* rose will be just about the shade we want."

"Well, I can find that, in good American paper, as I said before, at from thirty-seven to forty cents a roll. Then, our bordering : there 's an important question, for that must determine the carpet, the chairs, and everything else. Now what shall be the ground-tint of our rooms ? "

" There are only two to choose between," says the lady, — " green and marroon : which is the best for the picture ? "

" I think," says John, looking above the mantel-piece, as if he saw a picture there, — " I think a border of marroon velvet, with marroon furniture, is the best for the picture."

" I think so too," said she ; " and then we will have that lovely marroon and crimson carpet that I saw at Lowe's ; — it is an ingrain, to be sure, but has a Brussels pattern, a mossy, mixed figure, of different shades of crimson ; it has a good warm, strong color, and when I come to cover the lounges and our two old arm-chairs with marroon *rep*, it will make such a pretty effect."

" Yes," said John ; " and then, you know, our picture is so bright, it will light up the whole. Everything depends on the picture."

Now as to " the picture," it has a story must be told. John, having been all his life a worshipper and adorer of beauty and beautiful things, had never passed to or from his business without stopping at the print-shop windows, and seeing a little of what was there.

On one of these occasions he was smitten to the. heart with the beauty of an autumn landscape, where the red maples and sumachs, the purple and crimson oaks, all stood swathed and harmonized together in the hazy Indian-summer atmosphere. There was a great yellow chestnut-tree, on a distant hill, which stood out so naturally that John instinctively felt his fingers tingling for a basket, and his heels alive with a desire to bound over on to the rustling hillside and pick up the glossy brown nuts. Everything was there of autumn, even to the golden-rod and purple asters and scarlet creepers in the foreground.

John went in and inquired. It was by an unknown French artist, without name or patrons, who had just come to our shores to study our scenery, and this was the first picture he had exposed for sale. John had just been paid a quarter's salary; he bethought him of board-bill and washerwoman, sighed, and faintly offered fifty dollars.

To his surprise he was taken up at once, and the picture became his. John thought himself dreaming. He examined his treasure over and over, and felt sure that it was the work of no amateur beginner, but of a trained hand and a true artist-soul. So he found his way to the studio of the stranger, and apologized for having got such a gem for so much less than its worth. " It was all I *could* give, though," he said ; " and one

who paid four times as much could not value it more."
And so John took one and another of his friends, with
longer purses than his own, to the studio of the modest stranger ; and now his pieces command their full
worth in the market, and he works with orders far
ahead of his ability to execute, giving to the canvas
the traits of American scenery as appreciated and felt
by the subtile delicacy of the French mind, — our
rural summer views, our autumn glories, and the
dreamy, misty delicacy of our snowy winter land-
scapes. Whoso would know the truth of the same,
let him inquire for the modest studio of Morvillier,
at Malden, scarce a bow-shot from our Boston.

This picture had always been the ruling star of
John's house, his main dependence for brightening up
his bachelor-apartments ; and when he came to the
task of furbishing those same rooms for a fair occu-
pant, the picture was still his mine of gold. For a
picture, painted by a real artist, who studies Nature
minutely and conscientiously, has something of the
charm of the good Mother herself, — something of her
faculty of putting on different aspects under different
lights. John and his wife had studied their picture at
all hours of the day : they had seen how it looked
when the morning sun came aslant the scarlet maples
and made a golden shimmer over the blue mountains,
how it looked toned down in the cool shadows of after-

noon, and how it warmed up in the sunset, and died off mysteriously into the twilight; and now, when larger parlors were to be furnished, the picture was still the tower of strength, the rallying-point of their hopes.

"Do you know, John," said the wife, hesitating, "I am really in doubt whether we shall not have to get at least a few new chairs and a sofa for our parlors? They are putting in such splendid things at the other door that I am positively ashamed of ours; the fact is, they look almost disreputable, — like a heap of rubbish."

"Well," said John, laughing, "I don't suppose all together sent to an auction-room would bring us fifty dollars, and yet, such as they are, they answer the place of better things for us; and the fact is, Mary, the hard impassable barrier in the case is, that there really *is no money to get any more.*"

"Ah, well, then, if there is n't, we must see what we can do with these, and summon all the good fairies to our aid," said Mary. "There's your little cabinet-maker, John, will look over the things, and furbish them up; there's that broken arm of the chair must be mended, and everything revarnished; then I have found such a lovely *rep*, of just the richest shade of marroon, inclining to crimson, and when we come to cover the lounges and arm-chairs and sofas and ottomans all alike, you know they will be quite another thing."

"Trust you for that, Mary! By the by, I 've found a nice little woman, who has worked on upholstery, who will come in by the day, and be the hands that shall execute the decrees of your taste."

"Yes, I am sure we shall get on capitally. Do you know that I 'm almost glad we can't get new things? it 's a sort of enterprise to see what we can do with old ones."

"Now, you see, Mary," said John, seating himself on a lime-cask which the plasterers had left, and taking out his memorandum-book, "you see, I 've calculated this thing all over; I 've found a way by which I can make our rooms beautiful and attractive without a cent expended on new furniture."

"Well, let 's hear."

"Well, my way is short and simple. We must put things into our rooms that people will look at, so that they will forget to look at the furniture, and never once trouble their heads about it. People never look at furniture so long as there is anything else to look at ; just as Napoleon, when away on one of his expeditions, being told that the French populace were getting disaffected, wrote back, 'Gild the *dome des Invalides*,' and so they gilded it, and the people, looking at that, forgot everything else."

"But I'm not clear yet," said Mary, "what is coming of this rhetoric."

"Well, then, Mary, I'll tell you. A suit of new carved black-walnut furniture, severe in taste and perfect in style, such as I should choose at David and Saul's, could not be got under three hundred dollars, and I have n't the three hundred to give. What, then, shall we do? We must fall back on our resources; we must look over our treasures. We have our proof cast of the great glorious head of the Venus di Milo; we have those six beautiful photographs of Rome, that Brown brought to us; we have the great German lithograph of the San Sisto Mother and Child, and we have the two angel-heads, from the same; we have that lovely golden twilight sketch of Heade's; we have some sea-photographs of Bradford's; we have an original pen-and-ink sketch by Billings; and then, as before, we have 'our picture.' What has been the use of our watching at the gates and waiting at the doors of Beauty all our lives, if she has n't thrown us out a crust now and then, so that we might have it for time of need? Now, you see, Mary, we must make the toilet of our rooms just as a pretty woman makes hers when money runs low, and she sorts and freshens her ribbons, and matches them to her hair and eyes, and, with a bow here, and a bit of fringe there, and a button somewhere else, dazzles us into thinking that

she has an infinity of beautiful attire. Our rooms are
new and pretty of themselves, to begin with ; the tint
of the paper, and the rich coloring of the border,
corresponding with the furniture and carpets, will
make them seem prettier. And now for arrangement.
Take this front-room. I propose to fill those two
recesses each side of the fireplace with my books, in
their plain pine cases, just breast-high from the floor :
they are stained a good dark color, and nobody need
stick a pin in them to find out that they are not rose-
wood. The top of these shelves on either side to be
covered with the same stuff as the furniture, finished
with a crimson fringe. On top of the shelves on one
side of the fireplace I shall set our noble Venus di
Milo, and I shall buy at Cicci's the lovely Clytie, and
put it the other side. Then I shall get of Williams
and Everett two of their chromo-lithographs, which
give you all the style and charm of the best English
water-color school. I will have the lovely Bay of
Amalfi over my Venus, because she came from those
suns and skies of Southern Italy, and I will hang
Lake Como over my Clytie. Then, in the middle,
over the fireplace, shall be 'our picture.' Over each
door shall hang one of the lithographed angel-heads
of the San Sisto, to watch our going-out and coming-
in ; and the glorious Mother and Child shall hang
opposite the Venus di Milo, to show how Greek and

Christian unite in giving the noblest type to woman-hood. And then, when we have all our sketches and lithographs framed and hung here and there, and your flowers blooming as they always do, and your ivies wandering and rambling as they used to, and hanging in the most graceful ways and places, and all those little shells and ferns and vases, which you are always conjuring with, tastefully arranged, I 'll venture to say that our rooms will be not only pleasant, but beautiful, and that people will oftener say, ' How beautiful ! ' when they enter, than if we spent three times the money on new furniture."

In the course of a year after this conversation, one and another of my acquaintances were often heard speaking of John Merton's house. " Such beautiful rooms, — so charmingly furnished, — you must go and see them. What does make them so much pleasanter than those rooms in the other house, which have everything in them that money can buy ? " So said the folk, — for nine people out of ten only feel the effect of a room, and never analyze the causes from which it flows : they know that certain rooms seem dull and heavy and confused, but they don't know why ; that certain others seem cheerful, airy, and beautiful, but they know not why. The first excla-mation, on entering John's parlors, was so often, " How beautiful ! " that it became rather a byword

in the family.   Estimated by their mere money-value,
the articles in the rooms were of very trifling worth;
but as they stood arranged and combined, they had
all the effect of a lovely picture.   Although the statuary was only plaster, and the photographs and lithographs such as were all within the compass of limited
means, yet every one of them was a good thing of its
own kind, or a good reminder of some of the greatest
works of Art.   A good plaster cast is a daguerrotype,
so to speak, of a great statue, though it may be bought
for five or six dollars, while its original is not to be
had for any namable sum.   A chromo-lithograph of
the best sort gives all the style and manner and effect
of Turner or Stanfield, or any of the best of modern
artists, though you buy it for five or ten dollars, and
though the original would command a thousand guin-
eas.   The lithographs from Raphael's immortal picture give you the results of a whole age of artistic
culture, in a form within the compass of very humble
means.   There is now selling for five dollars at Williams and Everett's a photograph of Cheney's crayon
drawing of the San Sisto Madonna and Child, which
has the very spirit of the glorious original.   Such a
picture, hung against the wall of a child's room, would
train its eye from infancy; and yet how many will
freely spend five dollars in embroidery on its dress,
that say they cannot afford works of Art!

There was one advantage which John and his wife found in the way in which they furnished their house, that I have hinted at before : it gave freedom to their children. Though their rooms were beautiful, it was not with the tantalizing beauty of expensive and frail knick-knacks. Pictures hung against the wall, and statuary safely lodged on brackets, speak constantly to the childish eye, but are out of the reach of childish fingers, and are not upset by childish romps. They are not like china and crystal, liable to be used and abused by servants ; they do not wear out ; they are not spoiled by dust, nor consumed by moths. The beauty once there is always there ; though the mother be ill and in her chamber, she has no fears that she shall find it all wrecked and shattered. And this style of beauty, inexpensive as it is, compared with luxurious furniture, is a means of cultivation. No child is ever stimulated to draw or to read by an Axminster carpet or a carved centre-table ; but a room surrounded with photographs and pictures and fine casts suggests a thousand inquiries, stimulates the little eye and hand. The child is found with its pencil, drawing ; or he asks for a book on Venice, or wants to hear the history of the Roman Forum.

But I have made my article too long. I will write another on the moral and intellectual effects of house-furnishing.

"I have proved my point, Miss Jenny, have I not? *In house-furnishing, nothing is more economical than beauty.*"

"Yes, papa," said Jenny; "I give it up."

V.

RAKING UP THE FIRE.

WE have a custom at our house which we call *raking up the fire.* That is to say, the last half-hour before bedtime, we draw in, shoulder to shoulder, around the last brands and embers of our hearth, which we prick up and brighten, and dispose for a few farewell flickers and glimmers. This is a grand time for discussion. Then we talk over parties, if the young people have been out of an evening, — a book, if we have been reading one; we discuss and analyze characters, — give our views on all subjects, æsthetic, theological, and scientific, in a way most wonderful to hear; and, in fact, we sometimes get so engaged in our discussions that every spark of the fire burns out, and we begin to feel ourselves shivering around the shoulders, before we can remember that it is bedtime.

So, after the reading of my last article, we had a "raking-up talk," — to wit, Jenny, Marianne, and I, with Bob Stephens; — my wife, still busy at her work-basket, sat at the table a little behind us. Jenny, of course, opened the ball in her usual incisive manner.

"But now, papa, after all you say in your piece there, I cannot help feeling, that, if I had the taste and the money too, it would be better than the taste alone with no money. I like the nice arrangements and the books and the drawings; but I think all these would appear better still with really elegant furniture."

"Who doubts that?" said I. "Give me a large tub of gold coin to dip into, and the furnishing and beautifying of a house is a simple affair. The same taste that could make beauty out of cents and dimes could make it more abundantly out of dollars and eagles. But I have been speaking for those who have not, and cannot get, riches, and who wish to have agreeable houses; and I begin in the outset by saying that beauty is a thing to be respected, reverenced, and devoutly cared for, — and then I say that BEAUTY IS CHEAP, nay, to put it so that the shrewdest Yankee will understand it, BEAUTY IS THE CHEAPEST THING YOU CAN HAVE, because in many ways it is a substitute for expense. A few vases of flowers in a room, a few blooming, well-kept plants, a few prints framed in fanciful frames of cheap domestic fabric, a statuette, a bracket, an engraving, a pencil-sketch, above all, a few choice books, — all these arranged by a woman who has the gift in her finger-ends often produce such an illusion on the mind's eye that one goes away without once having noticed that the cushion of the armchair was worn out, and that some veneering had fallen off the centre-table.

"I have a friend, a schoolmistress, who lives in a poor little cottage enough, which, let alone of the Graces, might seem mean and sordid, but a few flower-seeds and a little weeding in the spring make it, all summer, an object which everybody stops to look at. Her æsthetic soul was at first greatly tried with the water-barrel which stood under the eaves-spout, — a most necessary evil, since only thus could her scanty supply of soft water for domestic purposes be secured. One of the Graces, however, suggested to her a happy thought. She planted a row of morning-glories round the bottom of her barrel, and drove a row of tacks around the top, and strung her water-butt with twine, like a great harpsichord. A few weeks covered the twine with blossoming plants, which every morning were a mass of many-colored airy blooms, waving in graceful sprays, and looking at themselves in the water. The water-barrel, in fact, became a celebrated stroke of ornamental gardening, which the neighbors came to look at."

"Well, but," said Jenny, "everybody has n't mamma's faculty with flowers. Flowers will grow for some people, and for some they won't. Nobody can see what mamma does so very much, but her plants always look fresh and thriving and healthy, — her things blossom just when she wants them, and do anything else she wishes them to ; and there are other people that fume and fuss and try, and their things won't do anything at all. There 's Aunt Easygo has plant after plant brought from the greenhouse, and hanging-baskets, and all sorts of things ; but her plants grow yellow and drop their leaves, and her hanging-baskets get dusty and poverty-stricken, while mamma's go on flourishing as heart could desire."

" I can tell you what your mother puts into her plants," said I, — " just what she has put into her children, and all her other home-things, — her *heart.* She *loves* them ; she lives in them ; she has in herself a plant-life and a plant-sympathy. She feels for them as if she herself were a plant ; she anticipates their wants, — always remembers them without an effort, and so the care flows to them daily and hourly. She hardly knows when she does the things that make them grow, — but she gives them a minute a hundred times a day. She moves this nearer the glass, — draws that back, — detects some thief of a worm on one, — digs at the root of another, to see why it droops, — washes these leaves, and sprinkles those, — waters, and refrains from watering, all with the habitual care of love. Your mother herself does n't know why her plants grow; it takes a philosopher and a writer for the 'Atlantic' to tell her what the cause is."

Here I saw my wife laughing over her work-basket as she answered, —

"Girls, one of these days, *I* will write an article for the 'Atlantic,' that your papa need not have *all* the say to himself: however, I believe he has hit the nail on the head this time."

"Of course he has," said Marianne. "But, mamma, I am afraid to begin to depend much on plants for the beauty of my rooms, for fear I should not have your gift, — and of all forlorn and hopeless things in a room, ill-kept plants are the most so."

"I would not recommend," said I, "a young house-keeper, just beginning, to rest much for her home ornament on plant-keeping, unless she has an experience of her own love and talent in this line, which makes her sure of success; for plants will not thrive, if they are forgotten or overlooked, and only tended in occasional intervals; and, as Marianne says, neglected plants are the most forlorn of all things."

"But, papa," said Marianne, anxiously, "there, in those patent parlors of John's that you wrote of, flowers acted a great part."

"The charm of those parlors of John's may be chemically analyzed," I said. "In the first place, there is sunshine, a thing that always affects the hu-

man nerves of happiness. Why else is it that people
are always so glad to see the sun after a long storm?
why are bright days matters of such congratulation?
Sunshine fills a house with a thousand beautiful and
fanciful effects of light and shade, — with soft, lumi-
nous, reflected radiances, that give picturesque effects
to the pictures, books, statuettes of an interior. John,
happily, had no money to buy brocatelle curtains, —
and besides this, he loved sunshine too much to buy
them, if he could. He had been enough with artists
to know that heavy damask curtains darken precisely
that part of the window where the light proper for
pictures and statuary should come in, namely, the upper part. The fashionable system of curtains lights
only the legs of the chairs and the carpets, and leaves
all the upper portion of the room in shadow. John's
windows have shades which can at pleasure be drawn
down from the top or up from the bottom, so that the
best light to be had may always be arranged for his
little interior."

"Well, papa," said Marianne, "in your chemical
analysis of John's rooms, what is the next thing to
the sunshine?"

"The next," said I, "is harmony of color. The
wall-paper, the furniture, the carpets, are of tints that
harmonize with one another. This is a grace in
rooms always, and one often neglected. The French

have an expressive phrase with reference to articles which are out of accord, — they say that they swear at each other. I have been in rooms where I seemed to hear the wall-paper swearing at the carpet, and the carpet swearing back at the wall-paper, and each article of furniture swearing at the rest. These appointments may all of them be of the most expensive kind, but with such dis-harmony no arrangement can ever produce anything but a vulgar and disagreeable effect. On the other hand, I have been in rooms where all the material was cheap, and the furniture poor, but where, from some instinctive knowledge of the reciprocal effect of colors, everything was harmonious, and produced a sense of elegance.

"I recollect once travelling on a Western canal through a long stretch of wilderness, and stopping to spend the night at an obscure settlement of a dozen houses. We were directed to lodgings in a common frame-house at a little distance, where, it seemed, the only hotel was kept. When we entered the parlor, we were struck with utter amazement at its prettiness, which affected us before we began to ask ourselves how it came to be pretty. It was, in fact, only one of the miracles of harmonious color working with very simple materials. Some woman had been busy there, who had both eyes and fingers. The sofa, the common wooden rocking-chairs, and some ottomans, probably made of old soap-boxes, were all covered with American nankeen of a soft yellowish-brown, with a bordering of blue print. The window-shades, the table-cover, and the piano-cloth, all repeated the same colors, in the same cheap material. A simple straw matting was laid over the floor, and, with a few books, a vase of flowers, and one or two prints, the room had a home-like, and even elegant air, that struck us all the more forcibly from its contrast with the usual tawdry, slovenly style of such parlors.

"The means used for getting up this effect were the most inexpensive possible, — simply the following-out, in cheap material, a law of uniformity and harmony, which always will produce beauty. In the same manner, I have seen a room furnished, whose effect was really gorgeous in color, where the only materials used were Turkey-red cotton and a simple ingrain carpet of corresponding color.

"Now, you girls have been busy lately in schemes for buying a velvet carpet for the new parlor that is to be, and the only points that have seemed to weigh in the council were that it was velvet, that it was cheaper than velvets usually are, and that it was a genteel pattern."

"Now, papa," said Jenny, "what ears you have! We thought you were reading all the time!"

"I see what you are going to say," said Marianne.

"You think that we have not once mentioned the consideration which should determine the carpet, — whether it will harmonize with our other things. But, you see, papa, we don't really know what our other things are to be."

"Yes," said Jenny, "and Aunt Easygo said it was an unusually good chance to get a velvet carpet."

"Yet, good as the chance is, it costs just twice as much as an ingrain."

"Yes, papa, it does."

"And you are not sure that the effect of it, after you get it down, will be as good as a well-chosen ingrain one."

"That's true," said Marianne, reflectively.

"But, then, papa," said Jenny, "Aunt Easygo said she never heard of such a bargain; only think, two dollars a yard for a *velvet!*"

"And why is it two dollars a yard? Is the man a personal friend, that he wishes to make you a present of a dollar on the yard? or is there some reason why it is undesirable?" said I.

"Well, you know, papa, he said those large patterns were not so salable."

"To tell the truth," said Marianne, "I never did like the pattern exactly; as to uniformity of tint, it might match with anything, for there's every color of the rainbow in it."

"You see, papa, it's a gorgeous flower-pattern," said Jenny.

"Well, Marianne, how many yards of this wonderfully cheap carpet do you want?"

"We want sixty yards for both rooms," said Jenny, always primed with statistics.

"That will be a hundred and twenty dollars," I said.

"Yes," said Jenny; "and we went over the figures together, and thought we could make it out by economizing in other things. Aunt Easygo said that the carpet was half the battle, — that it gave the air to everything else."

"Well, Marianne, if you want a man's advice in the case, mine is at your service."

"That is just what I want, papa."

"Well, then, my dear, choose your wall-papers and borderings, and, when they are up, choose an ingrain carpet to harmonize with them, and adapt your furniture to the same idea. The sixty dollars that you save on your carpet spend on engravings, chromolithographs, or photographs of some really *good* works of Art, to adorn your walls."

"Papa, I'll do it," said Marianne.

"My little dear," said I, "your papa may seem to be a sleepy old book-worm, yet he has his eyes open. Do you think I don't know why my girls have the credit of being the best-dressed girls on the street?"

"O papa!" cried out both girls in a breath.

"Fact, that!" said Bob, with energy, pulling at his mustache. "Everybody talks about your dress, and wonders how you make it out."

"Well," said I, "I presume you do not go into a shop and buy a yard of ribbon because it is selling at half-price, and put it on without considering complexion, eyes, hair, and shade of the dress, do you?"

"Of course we don't!" chimed in the duo, with energy.

"Of course you don't. Have n't I seen you mincing down-stairs, with all your colors harmonized, even to your gloves and gaiters? Now, a room must be dressed as carefully as a lady."

"Well, I'm convinced," said Jenny, "that papa knows how to make rooms prettier than Aunt Easygo; but then she said this was *cheap*, because it would outlast two common carpets."

"But, as you pay double price," said I, "I don't see that. Besides, I would rather, in the course of twenty years, have two nice, fresh ingrain carpets, of just the color and pattern that suited my rooms, than labor along with one ill-chosen velvet that harmonized with nothing."

"I give it up," said Jenny; "I give it up."

" Now, understand me," said I ; " I am not tra-
ducing velvet or Brussels or Axminster.   I admit that
more beautiful effects can be found in those goods than
in the humbler fabrics of the carpet-rooms.   Nothing
would delight me more than to put an unlimited credit
to Marianne's account, and let her work out the problems of harmonious color in velvet and damask.   All
I have to say is, that certain unities of color, certain
general arrangements, will secure very nearly as good
general effects in either material.   A library with a
neat, mossy green carpet on the floor, harmonizing
with wall-paper and furniture, looks generally as well,
whether the mossy green is made in Brussels or in
ingrain.   In the carpet-stores, these two materials
stand side by side in the very same pattern, and one
is often as good for the purpose as the other.   A lady
of my acquaintance, some years since, employed an
artist to decorate her parlors.   The walls being fres-
coed and tinted to suit his ideal, he immediately
issued his decree that her splendid velvet carpets
must be sent to auction, and others bought of certain
colors, harmonizing with the walls.   Unable to find
exactly the color and pattern he wanted, he at last
had the carpets woven in a neighboring factory, where,
as yet, they had only the art of weaving ingrains.
Thus was the material sacrificed at once to the harmony."

I remarked, in passing, that this was before Bigelow's mechanical genius had unlocked for America the higher secrets of carpet-weaving, and made it possible to have one's desires accomplished in Brussels or velvet. In those days, English carpet-weavers did not send to America for their looms, as they now do.

"But now to return to my analysis of John's rooms.

"Another thing which goes a great way towards giving them their agreeable air is the books in them. Some people are fond of treating books as others do children. One room in the house is selected, and every book driven into it and kept there. Yet nothing makes a room so home-like, so companionable, and gives it such an air of refinement, as the presence of books. They change the aspect of a parlor from that of a mere reception-room, where visitors perch for a transient call, and give it the air of a room where one feels like taking off one's things to stay. It gives the appearance of permanence and repose and quiet fellowship ; and next to pictures on the walls, the many-colored bindings and gildings of books are the most agreeable adornment of a room."

"Then, Marianne," said Bob, "we have something to start with, at all events. There are my English Classics and English Poets, and my uniform editions of Scott and Thackeray and Macaulay and Prescott and Irving and Longfellow and Lowell and Hawthorne

H

and Holmes and a host more. We really have something pretty there."

"You are a lucky girl," I said, "to have so much secured. A girl brought up in a house full of books, always able to turn to this or that author and look for any passage or poem when she thinks of it, does n't know what a blank a house without books might be."

"Well," said Marianne, "mamma and I were counting over my treasures the other day. Do you know, I have one really fine old engraving, that Bob says is quite a genuine thing ; and then there is that pencil-sketch that poor Schöne made for me the month before he died, — it is truly artistic."

"And I have a couple of capital things of Landseer's," said Bob.

"There 's no danger that your rooms will not be pretty," said I, "now you are fairly on the right track."

"But, papa," said Marianne, "I am troubled about one thing. My love of beauty runs into everything. I want pretty things for my table, — and yet, as you say, servants are so careless, one cannot use such things freely without great waste."

"For my part," said my wife, "I believe in best china, to be kept carefully on an upper-shelf, and taken down for high-days and holidays ; it may be a superstition, but I believe in it. It must never be taken out except when the mistress herself can see that it is safely cared for. My mother always washed her china herself; and it was a very pretty social ceremony, after tea was over, while she sat among us washing her pretty cups, and wiping them on a fine damask towel."

"With all my heart," said I; "have your best china, and venerate it,—it is one of the loveliest of domestic superstitions; only do not make it a bar to hospitality, and shrink from having a friend to tea with you, unless you feel equal to getting up to the high shelf where you keep it, getting it down, washing, and putting it up again.

"But in serving a table, I say, as I said of a house, beauty is a necessity, and beauty is cheap. Because you cannot afford beauty in one form, it does not follow that you cannot have it in another. Because one cannot afford to keep up a perennial supply of delicate china and crystal, subject to the accidents of raw, untrained servants, it does not follow that the every-day table need present a sordid assortment of articles chosen simply for cheapness, while the whole capacity of the purse is given to the set forever locked away for state-occasions.

"A table-service, all of simple white, of graceful forms, even though not of china, if arranged with care, with snowy, well-kept table-linen, clear glasses, and bright American plate in place of solid silver, may be made to look inviting ; add a glass of flowers every day, and your table may look pretty ; — and it is far more important that it should look pretty for the family every day than for company once in two weeks."

"I tell my girls," said my wife, "as the result of my experience, you may have your pretty china and your lovely fanciful articles for the table only so long as you can take all the care of them yourselves. As soon as you get tired of doing this, and put them into the hands of the trustiest servants, some good, well-meaning creature is sure to break her heart and your own and your very pet darling china pitcher all in one and the same minute ; and then her frantic despair leaves you not even the relief of scolding."

"I have become perfectly sure," said I, "that there are spiteful little brownies, intent on seducing good women to sin, who mount guard over the special idols of the china-closet. If you hear a crash, and a loud Irish wail from the inner depths, you never think of its being a yellow pie-plate, or that dreadful one-handled tureen that you have been wishing were broken these five years ; no, indeed, — it is sure to be the lovely painted china bowl, wreathed with morning-glories and sweet-peas, or the engraved glass goblet, with quaint old-English initials. China sacrificed must be a great means of saintship to women. Pope,

I think, puts it as the crowning grace of his perfect woman, that she is

> 'Mistress of herself, though china fall.'"

" I ought to be a saint by this time, then," said mamma ; " for in the course of my days I have lost so many idols by breakage, and peculiar accidents that seemed by a special fatality to befall my prettiest and most irreplaceable things, that in fact it has come to be a superstitious feeling now with which I regard anything particularly pretty of a breakable nature."

" Well," said Marianne, " unless one has a great deal of money, it seems to me that the investment in these pretty fragilities is rather a poor one."

" Yet," said I, " the principle of beauty is never so captivating as when it presides over the hour of daily meals. I would have the room where they are served one of the pleasantest and sunniest in the house. I would have its coloring cheerful, and there should be companionable pictures and engravings on the walls. Of all things, I dislike a room that seems to be kept like a restaurant, merely to eat in. I like to see in a dining-room something that betokens a pleasant sitting-room at other hours. I like there some books, a comfortable sofa or lounge, and all that should make it cosey and inviting. The custom in some families, of adoping for the daily meals one of the two parlors

which a city-house furnishes has often seemed to me
a particularly happy one. You take your meals, then,
in an agreeable place, surrounded by the little pleasant arrangements of your daily sitting-room ; and after
the meal, if the lady of the house does the honors of
her own pretty china herself, the office may be a pleasant and social one.

"But in regard to your table-service I have my
advice at hand. Invest in pretty table-linen, in delicate napkins, have your vase of flowers, and be guided
by the eye of taste in the choice and arrangement of
even the every-day table-articles, and have no ugly
things when you can have pretty ones by taking a
little thought. If you are sore tempted with lovely
china and crystal, too fragile to last, too expensive to
be renewed, turn away to a print-shop and comfort
yourself by hanging around the walls of your dining-
room beauty that will not break or fade, that will meet
your eye from year to year, though plates, tumblers,
and tea-sets successively vanish. There is my advice
for you, Marianne."

At the same time, let me say, in parenthesis, that
my wife, whose weakness is china, informed me that
night, when we were by ourselves, that she was ordering secretly a tea-set as a bridal gift for Marianne,
every cup of which was to be exquisitely painted with
the wild-flowers of America, from designs of her own,

— a thing, by the by, that can now be very nicely executed in our country, as one may find by looking in at
our friend Briggs's on School Street. "It will last her
all her life," she said, "and always be such a pleasure
to look at, — and a pretty tea-table is such a pretty
sight!" So spoke Mrs. Crowfield, "unweaned from
china by a thousand falls." She spoke even with tears
in her eyes. Verily, these women are harps of a thousand strings!

But to return to my subject.

"Finally and lastly," I said, "in my analysis and
explication of the agreeableness of those same parlors,
comes the crowning grace, — their *homeliness.* By
homeliness I mean not ugliness, as the word is apt to
be used, but the air that is given to a room by being
really at home in it. Not the most skilful arrangement can impart this charm.

"It is said that a king of France once remarked, —
' My son, you must seem to love your people.'

" ' Father, how shall I *seem* to love them?'

" ' My son, you *must* love them.'

"So to make rooms *seem* home-like you must be at
home in them. Human light and warmth are so wanting in some rooms, it is so evident that they are never
used, that you can never be at ease there. In vain
the house-maid is taught to wheel the sofa and turn
chair towards chair; in vain it is attempted to imitate
a negligent arrangement of the centre-table.

" Books that have really been read and laid down, chairs that have really been moved here' and there in the animation of social contact, have a sort of human vitality in them ; and a room in which people really live and enjoy is as different from a shut-up apartment as a live woman from a wax image.

" Even rooms furnished without taste often become charming from this one grace, that they seem to let you into the home-life and home-current. You seem to understand in a moment that you are taken into the family, and are moving in its inner circles, and not revolving at a distance in some outer court of the gentiles.

" How many people do we call on from year to year and know no more of their feelings, habits, tastes, family ideas and ways, than if they lived in Kamtschat-ka ! And why ? Because the room which they call a front-parlor is made expressly so that you never shall know. They sit in a back-room, — work, talk, read, perhaps. After the servant has let you in and opened a crack of the shutters, and while you sit waiting for them to change their dress and come in, you speculate as to what they may be doing. From some distant region, the laugh of a child, the song of a canary-bird, reaches you, and then a door claps hastily to. Do they love plants ? Do they write letters, sew, em-broider, crochet ? Do they ever romp and frolic ?

What books do they read? Do they sketch or paint?
Of all these possibilities the mute and muffled room
says nothing. A sofa and six chairs, two ottomans
fresh from the upholsterer's, a Brussels carpet, a centre-table with four gilt Books of Beauty on it, a mantel-
clock from Paris, and two bronze vases, — all these
tell you only in frigid tones, 'This is the best room,'
— only that, and nothing more, — and soon *she* trips
in in her best clothes, and apologizes for keeping you
waiting, asks how your mother is, and you remark that
it is a pleasant day, — and thus the acquaintance pro-
gresses from year to year. One hour in the little back-
room, where the plants and canary-bird and children
are, might have made you fast friends for life ; but as
it is, you care no more for them than for the gilt clock
on the mantel.

"And now, girls," said I, pulling a paper out of my
pocket, "you must know that your father is getting
to be famous by means of these 'House and Home
Papers.' Here is a letter I have just received : —

" ' MOST EXCELLENT MR. CROWFIELD, — Your
thoughts have lighted into our family-circle, and
echoed from our fireside. We all feel the force of
thém, and are delighted with the felicity of your treatment of the topic you have chosen. You have taken
hold of a subject that lies deep in our hearts, in a

6

genial, temperate, and convincing spirit. All must acknowledge the power of your sentiments upon their imaginations ;— if they could only trust to them in actual life ! There is the rub.

" 'Omitting further upon these points, there is a special feature of your articles upon which we wish to address you. You seem as yet (we do not know, of course, what you may hereafter do) to speak only of homes whose conduct depends upon the help of servants. Now your principles apply, as some of us well conceive, to nearly all classes of society ; yet most people, to take an impressive hint, must have their portraits drawn out more exactly. We therefore hope that you will give a reasonable share of your attention to us who do not employ servants, so that you may ease us of some of *our* burdens, which, in spite of common sense, we dare not throw off. For instance, we have company,—a friend from afar, (perhaps wealthy,) or a minister, or some other man of note. What do we do ? Sit down and receive our visitor with all good-will and the freedom of a home ? No ; we (the lady of the house) flutter about to clear up things, apologizing about this, that, and the other condition of unpreparedness, and, having settled the visitor in the parlor, set about marshalling the elements of a grand dinner or supper, such as no person but a gourmand wants to sit down to, when at home

and comfortable ; and in getting up this meal, clearing
away, and washing the dishes, we use up a good half
of the time which our guest spends with us. We have
spread ourselves, and shown him what we could do ;
but what a paltry, heart-sickening achievement ! Now,
good Mr. Crowfield, thou friend of the robbed and
despairing, wilt thou not descend into our purgatorial
circle, and tell the world what thou hast seen there of
doleful remembrance ? Tell us how we, who must do
and desire to do our own work, can show forth in our
homes a homely, yet genial hospitality, and entertain
our guests without making a fuss and hurly-burly, and
seeming to be anxious for their sake about many
things, and spending too much time getting meals,
as if eating were the chief social pleasure. *Won't* you
do this, Mr. Crowfield ?

> " ' Yours beseechingly,
> " ' R. H. A.' "

"That's a good letter," said Jenny.

"To be sure it is," said I.

"And shall you answer it, papa ? "

"In the very next 'Atlantic,' you may be sure I
shall. The class that do their own work are the
strongest, the most numerous, and, taking one thing
with another, quite as well cultivated a class as any
other. They are the anomaly of our country, — the

distinctive feature of the new society that we are building up here; and if we are to accomplish our national destiny, that class must increase rather than diminish. I shall certainly do my best to answer the very sensible and pregnant questions of that letter."

Here Marianne shivered and drew up a shawl, and Jenny gaped; my wife folded up the garment in which she had set the last stitch, and the clock struck twelve.

Bob gave a low whistle. "Who knew it was so late?"

"We have talked the fire fairly out," said Jenny.

V I.

THE LADY WHO DOES HER OWN WORK.

"MY dear Chris," said my wife, "is n't it time to be writing the next 'House and Home Paper'?"

I was lying back in my study-chair, with my heels luxuriously propped on an ottoman, reading for the two-hundredth time Hawthorne's "Mosses from an Old Manse," or his "Twice-Told Tales," I forget which, — I only know that these books constitute my cloud-land, where I love to sail away in dreamy quietude, forgetting the war, the price of coal and flour, the rates of exchange, and the rise and fall of gold. What do all these things matter, as seen from those enchanted gardens in Padua where the weird Rappaccini tends his enchanted plants, and his gorgeous daughter fills us with the light and magic of her presence, and saddens us with the shadowy allegoric mystery of her preternatural destiny? But my wife represents the positive forces of time, place, and number in our family, and, having also a chronological head, she knows the day of the month, and therefore gently reminded me that by inevitable dates the time drew near for preparing my — which is it now, May or June number?

"Well, my dear, you are right," I said, as by an exertion I came head-uppermost, and laid down the fascinating volume. "Let me see, what was I to write about?"

"Why, you remember you were to answer that letter from the lady who does her own work."

"Enough!" said I, seizing the pen with alacrity; "you have hit the exact phrase : —

"'The *lady* who *does her own work.*'"

America is the only country where such a title is possible, — the only country where there is a class of women who may be described as *ladies* who do their own work. By a lady we mean a woman of education, cultivation, and refinement, of liberal tastes and ideas, who, without any very material additions or changes, would be recognized as a lady in any circle of the Old World or the New.

What I have said is, that the existence of such a class is a fact peculiar to American society, a clear, plain result of the new principles involved in the doctrine of universal equality.

When the colonists first came to this country, of however mixed ingredients their ranks might have

been composed, and however imbued with the spirit
of feudal and aristocratic ideas, the discipline of the
wilderness soon brought them to a democratic level ;
the gentleman felled the wood for his log-cabin side
by side with the ploughman, and thews and sinews
rose in the market. "A man was deemed honorable
in proportion as he lifted his hand upon the high
trees of the forest." So in the interior domestic
circle. Mistress and maid, living in a log-cabin together, became companions, and sometimes the maid,
as the more accomplished and stronger, took prece-
dence of the mistress. It became natural and un-
avoidable that children should begin to work as early
as they were capable of it. The result was a generation of intelligent people brought up to labor from
necessity, but turning on the problem of labor the
acuteness of a disciplined brain. The mistress, out-
done in sinews and muscles by her maid, kept her
superiority by skill and contrivance. If she could
not lift a pail of water, she could invent methods
which made lifting the pail unnecessary, — if she
could not take a hundred steps without weariness,
she could make twenty answer the purpose of a hundred.

Slavery, it is true, was to some extent introduced
into New England, but it never suited the genius of
the people, never struck deep root, or spread so as to

choke the good seed of self-helpfulness. Many were
opposed to it from conscientious principle, — many
from far-sighted thrift, and from a love of thoroughness and well-doing which despised the rude, un-
skilled work of barbarians. People, having once felt
the thorough neatness and beauty of execution which
came of free, educated, and thoughtful labor, could
not tolerate the clumsiness of slavery. Thus it came
to pass that for many years the rural population of
New England, as a general rule, did their own work,
both out doors and in. If there were a black man or
black woman or bound girl, they were emphatically
only the *helps*, following humbly the steps of master
and mistress, and used by them as instruments of
lightening certain portions of their toil. The master and mistress with their children were the head
workers.

Great merriment has been excited in the Old Country, because years ago the first English travellers
found that the class of persons by them denominated
servants were in America denominated *help* or help-
ers. But the term was the very best exponent of the
state of society. There were few servants, in the
European sense of the word; there was a society of
educated workers, where all were practically equal,
and where, if there was a deficiency in one family
and an excess in another, a *helper*, not a servant, was

hired. Mrs. Browne, who has six sons and no daughters, enters into agreement with Mrs. Jones, who has six daughters and no sons. She borrows a daughter, and pays her good wages to help in her domestic toil, and sends a son to help the labors of Mr. Jones. These two young people go into the families in which they are to be employed in all respects as equals and companions, and so the work of the community is equalized. Hence arose, and for many years continued, a state of society more nearly solving than any other ever did the problem of combining the highest culture of the mind with the highest culture of the muscles and the physical faculties.

Then were to be seen families of daughters, handsome, strong females, rising each day to their in-door work with cheerful alertness, — one to sweep the room, another to make the fire, while a third prepared the breakfast for the father and brothers who were going out to manly labor; and they chatted meanwhile of books, studies, embroidery, discussed the last new poem, or some historical topic started by graver reading, or perhaps a rural ball that was to come off the next week. They spun with the book tied to the distaff; they wove; they did all manner of fine needlework; they made lace, painted flowers, and, in short, in the boundless consciousness of activity, invention, and perfect health, set themselves to any

6*

work they had ever read or thought of. A bride in
those days was married with sheets. and table-cloths
of her own weaving, with counterpanes and toilet-
covers wrought in divers embroidery by her own and
her sisters' hands. The amount of fancy-work done
in our days by girls who have nothing else to do will
not equal what was done by these, who performed besides, among them, the whole work of the family.

For many years these habits of life characterized
the majority of our rural towns.   They still exist
among a class respectable in numbers and position,
though perhaps not as happy in perfect self-satisfac-
tion and a conviction of the dignity and desirableness
of its lot as in former days.   Human nature is above
all things — lazy.   Every one confesses in the abstract that exertion which. brings out all the powers
of body and mind is the best thing for us all; but
practically most people do all they can to get rid of
it, and as a general rule nobody does much more than
circumstances drive him to do.   Even I would not
write this article, were not the publication-day hard
on my heels.   I should read Hawthorne and Emer-
son and Holmes, and dream in my arm-chair, and
project in the clouds those lovely unwritten stories
that curl and veer and change like mist-wreaths in the
sun.   So, also, however dignified, however invigorat-
ing, however really desirable are habits of life involv-

ing daily physical toil, there is a constant evil demon at every one's elbow, seducing him to evade it, or to bear its weight with sullen, discontented murmurs.

I will venture to say that there are at least, to speak very moderately, a hundred houses where these humble lines will be read and discussed, where there are no servants except the ladies of the household. I will venture to say, also, that these households, many of them, are not inferior in the air of cultivation and refined elegance to many which are conducted by the ministration of domestics. I will venture to assert, furthermore, that these same ladies who live thus find quite as much time for reading, letter-writing, drawing, embroidery, and fancy-work as the women of families otherwise arranged. I am quite certain that they would be found on an average to be in the enjoyment of better health, and more of that sense of capability and vitality which gives one confidence in one's ability to look into life and meet it with cheerful courage, than three quarters of the women who keep servants, — and that on the whole their domestic establishment is regulated more exactly to their mind, their food prepared and served more to their taste. And yet, with all this, I will *not* venture to assert that they are satisfied with this way of living, and that they would not change it forthwith, if they could. They have a secret feeling all the while that they are being abused, that they are working harder than they ought to, and that women who live in their houses like boarders, who have only to speak and it is done, are the truly enviable ones. One after another of their associates, as opportunity offers and means increase, deserts the ranks, and commits her domestic affairs to the hands of hired servants. Self-respect takes the alarm. Is it altogether genteel to live as we do? To be sure, we are accustomed to it; we have it all systematized and arranged; the work of our own hands suits us better than any we can hire; in fact, when we do hire, we are discontented and uncomfortable, — for who will do for us what we will do for ourselves? But when we have company! there's the rub, to get out all our best things and put them back, — to cook the meals and wash the dishes ingloriously, — and to make all appear as if we did n't do it, and had servants like other people.

There, after all, is the rub. A want of hardy self-respect, — an unwillingness to face with dignity the actual facts and necessities of our situation in life, — this, after all, is the worst and most dangerous feature of the case. It is the same sort of pride which makes Smilax think he must hire a waiter in white gloves, and get up a circuitous dinner-party on English principles, to entertain a friend from England. Because the friend in England lives in such and such a style, he must make believe for a day that he lives so too, when in fact it is a whirlwind in his domestic establishment equal to a removal or a fire, and threatens the total extinction of Mrs. Smilax. Now there are two principles of hospitality that people are very apt to overlook. One is, that their guests like to be made at home, and treated with confidence ; and another is, that people are always interested in the details of a way of life that is new to them. The Englishman comes to America as weary of his old, easy, family-coach life as you can be of yours ; he wants to see something new under the sun, — something American ; and forthwith we all bestir ourselves to give him something as near as we can fancy exactly like what he is already tired of. So city-people come to the country, not to sit in the best parlor, and to see the nearest imitation of city-life, but to lie on the hay-mow, to swing in the barn, to form intimacy with the pigs, chickens, and ducks, and to eat baked potatoes exactly on the critical moment when they are done, from the oven of the cooking-stove, — and we remark, *en passant*, that nobody has ever truly eaten a baked potato, unless he has seized it at that precise and fortunate moment.

I fancy you now, my friends, whom I have in my eye. You are three happy women together. You are all so well that you know not how it feels to be sick.

You are used to early rising, and would not lie in bed, if you could. Long years of practice have made you familiar with the shortest, neatest, most expeditious method of doing every household office, so that really for the greater part of the time in your house there seems to a looker-on to be nothing to do. You rise in the morning and despatch your husband, father, and brothers to the farm or wood-lot; you go sociably about chatting with each other, while you skim the milk, make the butter, turn the cheeses. The forenoon is long; it 's ten to one that all the so-called morning work is over, and you have leisure for an hour's sewing or reading before it is time to start the dinner preparations. By two o'clock your house-work is done, and you have the long afternoon for books, needlework, or drawing, — for perhaps there is among you one with a gift at her pencil. Perhaps one of you reads aloud while the others sew, and you manage in that way to keep up with a great deal of reading. I see on your book-shelves Prescott, Macaulay, Irving, besides the lighter fry of poems and novels, and, if I mistake not, the friendly covers of the "Atlantic." When you have company, you invite Mrs. Smith or Brown or Jones to tea; you have no trouble; they come early, with their knitting or sewing; your particular crony sits with you by your polished stove while you watch the baking of those light biscuits and tea-rusks

for which you are so famous, and Mrs. Somebody-
else chats with your sister, who is spreading the table
with your best china in the best room. When tea is
over, there is plenty of volunteering to help you wash
your pretty India teacups, and get them back into the
cupboard. There is no special fatigue or exertion in
all this, though you have taken down the best things
and put them back, because you have done all without
anxiety or effort, among those who would do precisely
the same, if you were their visitors.

But now comes down pretty Mrs. Simmons and her
pretty daughter to spend a week with you, and forthwith you are troubled. Your youngest, Fanny, visited
them in New York last fall, and tells you of their cook
and chambermaid, and the servant in white gloves that
waits on table. You say in your soul, "What shall we
do? they never can be contented to live as we do;
how shall we manage?" And now you long for servants.

This is the very time that you should know that
Mrs. Simmons is tired to death of her fine establishment, and weighed down with the task of keeping the
peace among her servants. She is a quiet soul, dearly
loving her ease, and hating strife; and yet last week
she had five quarrels to settle between her invaluable
cook and the other members of her staff, because
invaluable cook, on the strength of knowing how to get

up state-dinners and to manage all sorts of mysteries
which her mistress knows nothing about, asserts the
usual right of spoiled favorites to insult all her neighbors with impunity, and rule with a rod of iron over
the whole house.   Anything that is not in the least
like her own home and ways of living will be a blessed
relief and change to Mrs. Simmons.   Your clean, quiet
house, your delicate cookery, your cheerful morning
tasks, if you will let her follow you about, and sit
and talk with you while you are at your work, will
all seem a pleasant contrast to her own life.   Of
course, if it came to the case of offering to change
lots in life, she would not do it ; but very likely she
thinks she would, and sighs over and pities herself,
and thinks sentimentally how fortunate you are, how
snugly and securely you live, and wishes she were as
untrammelled and independent as you.   And she is
more than half right ; for, with her helpless habits,
her utter ignorance of the simplest facts concerning
the reciprocal relations of milk, eggs, butter, saleratus,
soda, and yeast, she is completely the victim and slave
of the person she pretends to rule.

Only imagine some of the frequent scenes and rehearsals in her family.   After many trials, she at last
engages a seamstress who promises to prove a perfect
treasure, — neat, dapper, nimble, skilful, and spirited.
The very soul of Mrs. Simmons rejoices in heaven.

Illusive bliss ! The new-comer proves to be no favorite with Madam Cook, and the domestic fates evolve
the catastrophe, as follows. First, low murmur of
distant thunder in the kitchen ; then a day or two of
sulky silence, in which the atmosphere seems heavy
with an approaching storm. At last comes the climax.
The parlor-door flies open during breakfast. Enter
seamstress, in tears, followed by Mrs. Cook with a
face swollen and red with wrath, who tersely intro-
duces the subject-matter of the drama in a voice trembling with rage.

" Would you be plased, Ma'am, to suit yerself with
another cook ? Me week will be up next Tuesday,
and I want to be going."

" Why, Bridget, what's the matter ? "

" Matter enough, Ma'am ! I niver could live with
them Cork girls in a house, nor I won't ; them as likes
the Cork girls is welcome for all me ; but it's not for
the likes of me to live with them, and she been in the
kitchen a-upsettin' of me gravies with her flat-irons
and things."

Here bursts in the seamstress with a whirlwind of
denial, and the altercation wages fast and furious, and
poor, little, delicate Mrs. Simmons stands like a kitten
in a thunder-storm in the midst of a regular Irish row.

Cook, of course, is sure of her victory. She knows
that a great dinner is to come off Wednesday, and

that her mistress has not the smallest idea how to
manage it, and that, therefore, whatever happens, she
must be conciliated.

Swelling with secret indignation at the tyrant, poor
Mrs. Simmons dismisses her seamstress with longing
looks. She suited her mistress exactly, but she did n't
suit cook !

Now, if Mrs. Simmons had been brought up in early
life with the experience that *you* have, she would be
mistress in her own house. She would quietly say
to Madam Cook, " If my family arrangements do not
suit you, you can leave. I can see to the dinner
myself." And she *could* do it. Her well-trained muscles would not break down under a little extra work ;
her skill, adroitness, and perfect familiarity with everything that is to be done would enable her at once to
make cooks of any bright girls of good capacity who
might still be in her establishment ; and, above all,
she would feel herself mistress in her own house.
This is what would come of an experience in doing
her own work as you do. She who can at once put
her own trained hand to the machine in any spot
where a hand is needed never comes to be the slave
of a coarse, vulgar Irishwoman.

So, also, in forming a judgment of what is to be
expected of servants in a given time, and what ought
to be expected of a given amount of provisions, poor

Mrs. Simmons is absolutely at sea. If even for one six months in her life she had been a practical cook, and had really had the charge of the larder, she would not now be haunted, as she constantly is, by an indefinite apprehension of an immense wastefulness, perhaps of the disappearance of provisions through secret channels of relationship and favoritism. She certainly could not be made to believe in the absolute necessity of so many pounds of sugar, quarts of milk, and dozens of eggs, not to mention spices and wine, as are daily required for the accomplishment of Madam Cook's purposes. But though now she does suspect and apprehend, she cannot speak with certainty. She cannot say, "*I* have made these things. I know exactly what they require. I have done this and that myself, and know it can be done, and done well, in a certain time." It is said that women who have been accustomed to doing their own work become hard mistresses. They are certainly more sure of the ground they stand on, — they are less open to imposition, — they can speak and act in their own houses more as those "having authority," and therefore are less afraid to exact what is justly their due, and less willing to endure impertinence and unfaithfulness. Their general error lies in expecting that any servant ever will do as well for them as they will do for themselves, and that an untrained, undisciplined human being ever *can* do house-work, or any other work, with the neatness and perfection that a person of trained intelligence can.   It has been remarked in our armies that the men of cultivation, though bred in delicate and refined spheres, can bear up under the hardships of camp-life better and longer than rough laborers. The reason is, that an educated mind knows how to use and save its body, to work it and spare it, as an uneducated mind cannot ; and so the college-bred youth brings himself safely through fatigues which kill the unreflective laborer.   Cultivated, intelligent women, who are brought up to do the work of their own families, are labor-saving institutions.   They make the head save the wear of the muscles.   By forethought, contrivance, system, and arrangement, they lessen the amount to be done, and do it with less expense of time and strength than others.   The old New England motto, *Get your work done up in the forenoon*, applied to an amount of work which would keep a common Irish servant toiling from daylight to sunset.

A lady living in one of our obscure New England towns, where there were no servants to be hired, at last by sending to a distant city succeeded in procuring a raw Irish maid-of-all-work, a creature of immense bone and muscle, but of heavy, unawakened brain. In one fortnight she established such a reign of Chaos and old Night in the kitchen and through the house, that her mistress, a delicate woman, encumbered with the care of young children, began seriously to think that she made more work each day than she performed, and dismissed her. What was now to be done? Fortunately, the daughter of a neighboring farmer. was going to be married in six months, and wanted a little ready money for her *trousseau*. The lady was informed that Miss So-and-so would come to her, not as a servant, but as hired "help." She was fain to accept any help with gladness. Forthwith came into the family-circle a tall, well-dressed young person, grave, unobtrusive, self-respecting, yet not in the least presuming, who sat at the family-table and observed all its decorums with the modest self-possession of a lady. The new-comer took a survey of the labors of a family of ten members, including four or five young children, and, looking, seemed at once to throw them into system, matured her plans, arranged her hours of washing, ironing, baking, cleaning, rose early, moved deftly, and in a single day the slatternly and littered kitchen assumed that neat, orderly appearance that so often strikes one in New England farm-houses. The work seemed to be all gone. Everything was nicely washed, brightened, put in place, and stayed in place; the floors, when cleaned, remained clean; the work was always done, and not

doing ; and every afternoon the young lady sat neatly
dressed in her own apartment, either quietly writing
letters to her betrothed, or sewing on her bridal outfit.
Such is the result of employing those who have been
brought up to do their own work. That tall, fine-look-
ing girl, for aught we know, may yet be mistress of a
fine house on Fifth Avenue ; and if she is, she will,
we fear, prove rather an exacting mistress to Irish
Biddy and Bridget ; but *she* will never be threatened
by her cook and chambermaid, after the first one or
two have tried the experiment.

Having written thus far on my article, I laid it
aside till evening, when, as usual, I was saluted by
the inquiry, " Has papa been writing anything to-
day ? " and then followed loud petitions to hear it ;
and so I read as far, reader, as you have.

" Well, papa," said Jenny, " what are you meaning
to make out there ?   Do you really think it would be
best for us all to try to go back to that old style of
living you describe ?   After all, you have shown only
the dark side of an establishment with servants, and
the bright side of the other way of living.   Mamma
does not have such trouble with her servants ; matters
have always gone smoothly in our family ; and if we
are not such wonderful girls as those you describe,
yet we may make pretty good housekeepers on the
modern system, after all."

" You don't know all the troubles your mamma has had in your day," said my wife. " I have often, in the course of my family-history, seen the day when I have heartily wished for the strength and ability to manage my household matters as my grandmother of notable memory managed hers. But I fear that those remarkable women of the olden times are like the ancient painted glass, — the art of making them is lost ; my mother was less than her mother, and I am less than my mother."

"And Marianne and I come out entirely at the little end of the horn," said Jenny, laughing ; " yet I wash the breakfast-cups and dust the parlors, and have always fancied myself a notable housekeeper."

" It is just as I told you," I said. " Human nature is always the same. Nobody ever is or does more than circumstances force him to be and do. Those remarkable women of old were made by circumstances. There were, comparatively speaking, no servants to be had, and so children were trained to habits of industry and mechanical adroitness from the cradle, and every household process was reduced to the very minimum of labor. Every step required in a process was counted, every movement calculated ; and she who took ten steps, when one would do, lost her reputation for 'faculty.' Certainly such an early drill was of use in developing the health and the bodily powers, as well as in giving precision to the practical mental faculties. All household economies were arranged with equal niceness in those thoughtful minds. A trained housekeeper knew just how many sticks of hickory of a certain size were required to heat her oven, and how many of each different kind of wood. She knew by a sort of intuition just what kinds of food would yield the most palatable nutriment with the least outlay of accessories in cooking. She knew to a minute the time when each article must go into and be withdrawn from her oven; and if she could only lie in her chamber and direct, she could guide an intelligent child through the processes with mathematical certainty. It is impossible, however, that anything but early training and long experience can produce these results, and it is earnestly to be wished that the grandmothers of New England had only written down their experiences for our children; they would have been a mine of maxims and traditions, better than any other traditions of the elders which we know of."

"One thing I know," said Marianne, — "and that is, I wish I had been brought up so, and knew all that I should; and had all the strength and adroitness that those women had. I should not dread to begin housekeeping, as I now do. I should feel myself independent. I should feel that I knew how to direct my servants, and what it was reasonable and proper to

expect of them ; and then, as you say, I should n't
be dependent on all their whims and caprices of temper. I dread those household storms, of all things."

Silently pondering these anxieties of the young
expectant housekeeper, I resumed my pen, and con-
cluded my paper as follows.

In this country, our democratic institutions have
removed the superincumbent pressure which in the
Old World confines the servants to a regular orbit.
They come here feeling that this is somehow a land
of liberty, and with very dim and confused notions of
what liberty is. They are for the most part the raw,
untrained Irish peasantry, and the wonder is, that,
with all the unreasoning heats and prejudices of the
Celtic blood, all the necessary ignorance and rawness,
there should be the measure of comfort and success
there is in our domestic arrangements. But, so long
as things are so, there will be constant changes and
interruptions in every domestic establishment, and
constantly recurring interregnums when the mistress
must put her own hand to the work, whether the hand
be a trained or an untrained one. As matters now
are, the young housekeeper takes life at the hardest.
She has very little strength, — no experience to teach
her how to save her strength. She knows nothing
experimentally of the simplest processes necessary to

keep her family comfortably fed and clothed; and she has a way of looking at all these things which makes them particularly hard and distasteful to her. She does not escape being obliged to do house-work at intervals, but she does it in a weak, blundering, confused way, that makes it twice as hard and disagreeable as it need be.

Now what I have to say is, that, if every young woman learned to do house-work and cultivated her practical faculties in early life, she would, in the first place, be much more likely to keep her servants, and, in the second place, if she lost them temporarily, would avoid all that wear and tear of the nervous system which comes from constant ill-success in those departments on which family health and temper mainly depend. This is one of the peculiarities of our American life which require a peculiar training. Why not face it sensibly?

The second thing I have to say is, that our land is now full of motorpathic institutions to which women are sent at great expense to have hired operators stretch and exercise their inactive muscles. They lie for hours to have their feet twigged, their arms flexed, and all the different muscles of the body worked for them, because they are so flaccid and torpid that the powers of life do not go on. Would it not be quite as cheerful and less expensive a process, if young girls from early life developed the muscles in sweeping, dusting, ironing, rubbing furniture, and all the multiplied domestic processes which our grandmothers knew of? A woman who did all these, and diversified the intervals with spinning on the great and little wheel, never came to need the gymnastics of Dio Lewis or of the Swedish motorpathist, which really are a necessity now. Does it not seem poor economy to pay servants for letting our muscles grow feeble, and then to pay operators to exercise them for us? I will venture to say that our grandmothers in a week went over every movement that any gymnast has invented, and went over them to some productive purpose too.

Lastly, my paper will not have been in vain, if those ladies who have learned and practise the invaluable accomplishment of doing their own work will know their own happiness and dignity, and properly value their great acquisition, even though it may have been forced upon them by circumstances.

VII.

WHAT CAN BE GOT IN AMERICA.

WHILE I was preparing my article for the "Atlantic," our friend Bob Stephens burst in upon us, in some considerable heat, with a newspaper in his hand.

"Well, girls, your time is come now! You women have been preaching heroism and sacrifice to us, — 'so splendid to go forth and suffer and die for our country,' — and now comes the test of feminine patriotism."

"Why, what's the matter now?" said Jenny, running eagerly to look over his shoulder at the paper.

"No more foreign goods," said he, waving it aloft, — "no more gold shipped to Europe for silks, laces, jewels, kid gloves, and what-not. Here it is, — great movement, headed by senators' and generals' wives, Mrs. General Butler, Mrs. John P. Hale, Mrs. Henry Wilson, and so on, a long string of them, to buy no more imported articles during the war."

"But I don't see how it *can* be done," said Jenny.

"Why," said I, "do you suppose that 'nothing to wear' is made in America?"

"But, dear Mr. Crowfield," said Miss Featherstone, a nice girl, who was just then one of our family-circle, "there is not, positively, much that is really fit to use or wear made in America, — *is* there now? Just think; how is Marianne to furnish her house here without French papers and English carpets? — those American papers are so very ordinary, and as to American carpets, everybody knows their colors don't hold; and then, as to dress, a lady must have gloves, you know, — and everybody knows no such things are made in America as gloves."

"I think," I said, "that I have heard of certain fair ladies wishing that they were men, that they might show with what alacrity they would sacrifice everything on the altar of their country: life and limb would be nothing; they would glory in wounds and bruises, they would enjoy losing a right arm, they would n't mind limping about on a lame leg the rest of their lives, *if they were John or Peter*, if only they might serve their dear country."

"Yes," said Bob, "that's female patriotism! Girls are always ready to jump off from precipices, or throw themselves into abysses, but as to wearing an unfashionable hat or thread gloves, that they can't do, — not even for their dear country. No matter whether there's any money left to pay for the war or not, the dear souls must have twenty yards of silk in a dress, — it's the fashion, you know."

" Now, is n't he too bad ? " said Marianne. "As if we 'd ever been asked to make these sacrifices and refused ! I think I have seen women ready to give up dress and fashion and everything else, for a good cause."

" For that matter," said I, " the history of all wars has shown women ready to sacrifice what is most intimately feminine in times of peril to their country. The women of Carthage not only gave up their jewels in the siege of their city, but, in the last extremity, cut off their hair for bow-strings.   The women of Hungary and Poland, in their country's need, sold their jewels and plate and wore ornaments of iron and lead. In the time of our own Revolution, our women dressed in plain homespun and drank herb-tea, — and certainly nothing is more feminine than a cup of tea. And in this very struggle, the women of the Southern States have cut up their carpets for blankets, have borne the most humiliating retrenchments and privations of all kinds without a murmur.   So let us exonerate the female sex of want of patriotism, at any rate."

" Certainly," said my wife ; " and if our Northern women have not retrenched and made sacrifices, it has been because it has not been impressed on them that there is any particular call for it.   Everything has seemed to be so prosperous and plentiful in the Northern States, money has been so abundant and easy to come by, that it has really been difficult to realize that a dreadful and destructive war was raging. Only occasionally, after a great battle, when the lists of the killed and wounded have been sent through the country, have we felt that we were making a sacrifice. The women who have spent such sums for laces and jewels and silks have not had it set clearly before them why they should not do so. The money has been placed freely in their hands, and the temptation before their eyes."

"Yes," said Jenny, "I am quite sure that there are hundreds who have been buying foreign goods, who would not do it, if they could see any connection between their not doing it and the salvation of the country; but when I go to buy a pair of gloves, I naturally want the best pair I can find, the pair that will last the longest and look the best, and these always happen to be French gloves."

"Then," said Miss Featherstone, "I never could clearly see why people should confine their patronage and encouragement to works of their own country. I'm sure the poor manufacturers of England have shown the very noblest spirit with relation to our cause, and so have the silk-weavers and artisans of France,—at least, so I have heard; why should we not give them a fair share of encouragement, particularly when they make things that we are not in circumstances to make, have not the means to make ? "

" Those are certainly sensible questions," I replied, " and ought to meet a fair answer, and I should say, that, were our country in a fair ordinary state of prosperity, there would be no reason why our wealth should not flow out for the encouragement of well-directed industry in any part of the world ; from this point of view we might look on the whole world as our country, and cheerfully assist in developing its wealth and resources. But our country is now in the situation of a private family whose means are absorbed by an expensive sickness, involving the life of its head ; just now it is all we can do to keep the family together, all our means are swallowed up by our own domestic wants, we have nothing to give for the encouragement of other families, we must exist ourselves, we must get through this crisis and hold our own, and that we may do it all the family expenses must be kept within ourselves as far as possible. If· we drain off all the gold of the country to send to Europe to encourage her worthy artisans, we produce high prices and distress among equally worthy ones at home, and we lessen the amount of our resources for maintaining the great struggle for national existence. The same amount of money which we pay for foreign luxuries, if passed into the hands of our own manufacturers and producers, becomes available for the increasing expenses of the war."

"But, papa," said Jenny, "I understood that a great part of our Governmental income was derived from the duties on foreign goods, and so I inferred that the more foreign goods were imported the better it would be."

"Well, suppose," said I, "that for every hundred thousand dollars we send out of the country we pay the Government ten thousand; that is about what our gain as a nation would be;—we send our gold abroad in a great stream, and give our Government a little driblet."

"Well, but," said Miss Featherstone, "*what can be got in America?* Hardly anything, I believe, except common calicoes."

"Begging your pardon, my dear lady," said I, "there is where you and multitudes of others are greatly mistaken. Your partiality for foreign things has kept you ignorant of what you have at home. Now I am not blaming the love of foreign things; it is not peculiar to us Americans; all nations have it. It is a part of the poetry of our nature to love what comes from afar, and reminds us of lands distant and different from our own. The English belles seek after French laces; the French beauty enumerates English laces among her rarities; and the French dandy piques himself upon an English tailor. We Americans are great travellers, and few people travel, I fancy, with more real enjoyment than we ; our domestic establishments, as compared with those of the Old World, are less cumbrous and stately, and so our money is commonly in hand as pocket-money, to be spent freely and gayly in our tours abroad.

"We have such bright and pleasant times in every country that we conceive a kindliness for its belongings. To send to Paris for our dresses and our shoes and our gloves may not be a mere bit of foppery, but a reminder of the bright, pleasant hours we have spent in that city of Boulevards and fountains. Hence it comes, in a way not very blamable, that many people have been so engrossed with what can be got from abroad that they have neglected to inquire what can be found at home ; they have supposed, of course, that to get a decent watch they must send to Geneva or to London, — that to get thoroughly good carpets they must have the English manufacture, — that a really tasteful wall-paper could be found only in Paris, — and that flannels and broadcloths could come only from France, Great Britain, or Germany."

"Well, is n't it so ?" said Miss Featherstone. "I certainly have always thought so ; I never heard of American watches, I 'm sure."

"Then," said I, "I 'm sure you can't have read an

article that you should have read on the Waltham
watches, written by our friend George W. Curtis, in
the "Atlantic" for January of last year. I must refer
you to that to learn that we make in America watches
superior to those of Switzerland or England, bringing
into the service machinery and modes of workmanship unequalled for delicacy and precision ; as I said
before, you must get the article and read it, and if
some sunny day you could make a trip to Waltham,
and see the establishment, it would greatly assist your
comprehension."

"Then, as to men's clothing," said Bob, "I know
to my entire satisfaction that many of the most popu-
lar cloths for men's wear are actually American fabrics
baptized with French and English names to make
them sell."

"Which shows," said I, "the use of a general community movement to employ American goods. It will
change the fashion. The demand will create the supply. When the leaders of fashion are inquiring for
American instead of French and English fabrics, they
will be surprised to find what nice American articles
there are. The work of our own hands will no more
be forced to skulk into the market under French and
English names, and we shall see, what is really true,
that an American gentleman need not look beyond
his own country for a wardrobe befitting him. I am

positive that we need not seek broadcloth or other woollen goods from foreign lands, — that *better* hats are made in America than in Europe, and better boots and shoes ; and I should be glad to send an American gentleman to the World's Fair dressed from top to toe in American manufactures, with an American watch in his pocket, and see if he would suffer in comparison with the gentlemen of any other country."

"Then, as to house-furnishing," began my wife, "American carpets are getting to be every way equal to the English."

"Yes," said I, "and what is more, the Brussels carpets of England are woven on looms invented by an American, and bought of him. Our countryman, Bigelow, went to England to study carpet-weaving in the English looms, — supposing that all arts were generously open for the instruction of learners. He was denied the opportunity of studying the machinery and watching the processes by a short-sighted jealousy. He immediately sat down with a yard of carpeting, and, patiently unravelling it, thread by thread, combined and calculated till he invented the machinery on which the best carpets of the Old and New World are woven. No pains which such ingenuity and energy can render effective are spared to make our fabrics equal those of the British market, and we need only to be disabused of the old prejudice, and to keep up

with the movement of our own country, and find out
our own resources.   The fact is, every year improves
our fabrics.   Our mechanics, our manufacturers, are
working with an energy, a zeal, and a skill that carry
things forward faster than anybody dreams of; and
nobody can predicate the character of American articles, in any department, now, by their character even
five years ago."

"Well, as to wall-papers," said Miss Featherstone,
"there you must confess the French are and must be
unequalled."

"I do not confess any such thing," said I, hardily.
"I grant you that in that department of paper-hangings
which exhibits floral decoration the French designs
and execution are and must be for some time to come
far ahead of all the world, — their drawing of flowers,
vines, and foliage has the accuracy of botanical studies
and the grace of finished works of art, and we cannot
as yet pretend in America to do anything equal to it.
But for satin finish, and for a variety of exquisite tints
of plain colors, American papers equal any in the
world ; our gilt papers even surpass in the heaviness
and polish of the gilding those of foreign countries ;
and we have also gorgeous velvets.   All I have to say
is, let people who are furnishing houses inquire for
articles of American manufacture, and they will be
surprised at what they will see.   We need go no

farther than our Cambridge glass-works to see that
the most dainty devices of cut-glass, crystal, ground
and engraved glass of every color and pattern, may be
had of American workmanship, every way equal to
the best European make, and for half the price.   And
American painting on china is so well executed both
in Boston and New York, that deficiencies in the finest
French or English sets can be made up in a style not
distinguishable from the original, as one may easily
see by calling on our worthy next neighbor, Briggs, who
holds the opposite corner to our "Atlantic Monthly."
No porcelain, it is true, is yet made in America,
these decorative arts being exercised on articles imported from Europe.   Our tables must, therefore, per
force, be largely indebted to foreign lands for years
to come.   Exclusive of this item, however, I believe
it would require very little self-denial to paper, carpet,
and furnish a house entirely from the manufactures
of America.   I cannot help saying one word here in
favor of the cabinet-makers of Boston.   There is so
much severity of taste, such a style and manner about
the best made Boston furniture, as raises it really quite
into the region of the fine arts.   Our artisans have
studied foreign models with judicious eyes, and so
transferred to our country the spirit of what is best
worth imitating, that one has no need to import furniture from Europe."

"Well," said Miss Featherstone, "there is one point you cannot make out, — gloves; certainly the French have the monopoly of that article."

"I am not going to ruin my cause by asserting too much," said I. "I have n't been with nicely dressed women so many years not to speak with proper respect of Alexander's gloves, — and I confess, honestly, that to forego them must be a fair, square sacrifice to patriotism. But then, on the other hand, it is nevertheless true that gloves have long been made in America and surreptitiously brought into market as French. I have lately heard that very nice kid gloves are made at Watertown and in Philadelphia. I have only heard of them, and not seen. A loud demand might bring forth an unexpected supply from these and other sources. If the women of America were bent on having gloves made in their own country, how long would it be before apparatus and factories would spring into being? Look at the hoop-skirt factories, — women wanted hoop-skirts, — would have them or die, — and forthwith factories arose, and hoop-skirts became as the dust of the earth for abundance."

"Yes," said Miss Featherstone, "and, to say the truth, the American hoop-skirts are the only ones fit to wear. When we were living on the Champs Élysées, I remember we searched high and low for something like them, and finally had to send home to America for some."

"Well," said I, "that shows what I said. Let there be only a hearty call for an article, and it will come. These spirits of the vasty deep are not so very far off, after all, as we may imagine, and women's unions and leagues will lead to inquiries and demands which will as infallibly bring supplies as a vacuum will create a draught of air."

"But, at least, there are no ribbons made in America," said Miss Featherstone.

"Pardon, my lady, there is a ribbon-factory now in operation in Boston, and ribbons of every color are made in New York; there is also in the vicinity of Boston a factory which makes Roman scarfs. This shows that the faculty of weaving ribbons is not wanting to us Americans, and a zealous patronage would increase the supply.

"Then, as for a thousand and one little feminine needs, I believe our manufacturers can supply them. The Portsmouth Steam Company makes white spool-cotton equal to any in England, and colored spool-cotton, of every shade and variety, such as is not made either in England or France. Pins are well made in America; so are hooks and eyes, and a variety of buttons. Straw bonnets of American manufacture are also extensively in market, and quite as pretty ones as the double-priced ones which are imported.

"As to silks and satins, I am not going to pretend

that they are to be found here. It is true, there are silk manufactories, like that of the Cheneys in Connecticut, where very pretty foulard dress-silks are made, together with sewing-silk enough to supply a large demand. Enough has been done to show that silks might be made in America; but at present, as compared with Europe, we claim neither silks nor thread laces among our manufactures.

"But what then? These are not necessaries of life. Ladies can be very tastefully dressed in other fabrics besides silks. There are many pretty American dress-goods which the leaders of fashion might make fashionable; and certainly no leader of fashion could wish to dress for a nobler object than to aid her country in deadly peril.

"It is not a life-pledge, not a total abstinence, that is asked, — only a temporary expedient to meet a stringent crisis. We only ask a preference for American goods where they can be found. Surely, women whose exertions in Sanitary Fairs have created an era in the history of the world will not shrink from so small a sacrifice for so obvious a good.

"Here is something in which every individual woman can help. Every woman who goes into a shop and asks for American goods renders an appreciable aid to our cause. She expresses her opinion and her patriotism; and her voice forms a part of that demand which shall arouse and develop the resources of her country. We shall learn to know our own country. We shall learn to respect our own powers, — and every branch of useful labor will spring and flourish under our well-directed efforts. We shall come out of our great contest, not bedraggled, ragged, and poverty-stricken, but developed, instructed, and rich. Then will we gladly join with other nations in the free interchange of manufactures, and gratify our eye and taste with what is foreign, while we can in turn send abroad our own productions in equal ratio."

"Upon my word," said Miss Featherstone, "I should think it was the Fourth of July, — but I yield the point. I am convinced ; and henceforth you will see me among the most stringent of the leaguers."

"Right !" said I.

And, fair lady-reader, let me hope you will say the same. You can do something for your country, — it lies right in your hand. Go to the shops, determined on supplying your family and yourself with American goods. Insist on having them ; raise the question of origin over every article shown to you. In the Revolutionary times, some of the leading matrons of New England gave parties where the ladies were dressed in homespun and drank sage-tea. Fashion makes all things beautiful, and you, my charming and accomplished friend, can create beauty by creating fashion.

What makes the beauty of half the Cashmere shawls? Not anything in the shawls themselves, for they often look coarse and dingy and barbarous. It is the association with style and fashion. Fair lady, give style and fashion to the products of your own country, — resolve that the money in your hand shall go to your brave brothers, to your co-Americans, now straining every nerve to uphold the nation, and cause it to stand high in the earth. What are you without your country? As Americans you can hope for no rank but the rank of your native land, no badge of nobility but her beautiful stars. It rests with this conflict to decide whether those stars shall be badges of nobility to you and your children in all lands. Women of America, your country expects every woman to do her duty!

VIII.

ECONOMY.

" THE fact is," said Jenny, as she twirled a little
hat on her hand, which she had been making
over, with nobody knows what of bows and pompons,
and other matters for which the women have curious
names, — "the fact is, American women and girls
must learn to economize ; it is n't merely restricting
one's self to American goods, it is general economy,
that is required. Now here 's this hat, — costs me
only three dollars, all told ; and Sophie Page bought
an English one this morning at Madame Meyer's for
which she gave fifteen. And I really don't think hers
has more of an air than mine. I made this over, you
see, with things I had in the house, bought nothing
but the ribbon, and paid for altering and pressing,
and there you see what a stylish hat I have ! "

" Lovely ! admirable ! " said Miss Featherstone.
" Upon my word, Jenny, you ought to marry a poor
parson ; you would be quite thrown away upon a rich
man."

" Let me see," said I. " I want to admire intelligently. That is n't the hat you were wearing yester-day?"

"O no, papa! This is just done. The one I wore yesterday was my waterfall-hat, with the green feather; this, you see, is an oriole."

"A what?"

"An oriole. Papa, how can you expect to learn about these things?"

"And that plain little black one, with the stiff crop of scarlet feathers sticking straight up?"

"That 's my jockey, papa, with a plume *en militaire.*"

"And did the waterfall and the jockey cost anything?"

"They were very, very cheap, papa, all things considered. Miss Featherstone will remember that the waterfall was a great bargain, and I had the feather from last year; and as to the jockey, that was made out of my last year's white one, dyed over. You know, papa, I always take care of my things, and they last from year to year."

"I do assure you, Mr. Crowfield," said Miss Featherstone, "I never saw such little economists as your daughters; it is perfectly wonderful what they contrive to dress on. How they manage to do it I 'm sure I can't see. I never could, I 'm convinced."

"Yes," said Jenny, "I' ve bought but just one new

hat. I only wish you could sit in church where we do, and see those Miss Fielders. Marianne and I have counted six new hats apiece of those girls', — *new*, you know, just out of the milliner's shop ; and last Sunday they came out in such lovely puffed tulle bonnets ! Were n't they lovely, Marianne ? And next Sunday, I don't doubt, there 'll be something else."

"Yes," said Miss Featherstone, — "their father, they say, has made a million dollars lately on Government contracts."

"For my part," said Jenny, "I think such extravagance, at such a time as this, is shameful."

"Do you know," said I, "that I 'm quite sure the Misses Fielder think they are practising rigorous economy ? "

"Papa ! Now there you are with your paradoxes ! How can you say so ? "

"I should n't be afraid to bet a pair of gloves, now," said I, "that Miss Fielder thinks herself half ready for translation, because she has bought only six new hats and a tulle bonnet so far in the season. If it were not for her dear bleeding country, she would have had thirty-six, like the Misses Sibthorpe. If we were admitted to the secret councils of the Fielders, doubtless we should perceive what temptations they daily resist ; how perfectly rubbishy and dreadful they suffer themselves to be, because they feel it important

now, in this crisis, to practise economy; how they
abuse the Sibthorpes, who have a new hat every time
they drive out, and never think of wearing one more
than two or three times; how virtuous and self-deny-
ing they feel, when they think of the puffed tulle, for
which they only gave eighteen dollars, when Madame
Caradori showed them those lovely ones, like the
Misses Sibthorpe's, for forty-five; and how they go
home descanting on virgin simplicity, and resolving
that they will not allow themselves to be swept into
the vortex of extravagance, whatever other people
may do."

"Do you know," said Miss Featherstone, "I believe your papa is right? I was calling on the oldest
Miss Fielder the other day, and she told me that she
positively felt ashamed to go looking as she did, but
.that she really did feel the necessity of economy.
'Perhaps we might afford to spend more than some
others,' she said; 'but it's so much better to give the
money to the Sanitary Commission!'"

"Furthermore," said I, "I am going to put forth
another paradox, and say that very likely there are
some people looking on my girls, and commenting
on them for extravagance in having three hats, even
though made over, and contrived from last year's
stock."

"They can't know anything about it, then," said

Jenny, decisively; "for, certainly, nobody can be decent, and invest less in millinery than Marianne and I do."

"When I was a young lady," said my wife, "a well-dressed girl got her a new bonnet in the spring, and another in the fall ; — that was the extent of her purchases in this line. A second-best bonnet, left of last year, did duty to relieve and preserve the best one. My father was accounted well-to-do, but I had no more, and wanted no more. I also bought myself, every spring, two pair of gloves, a dark and a light pair, and wore them through the summer, and another two through the winter ; one or two pair of white kids, carefully cleaned, carried me through all my parties. Hats had not been heard of, and the great necessity which requires two or three new ones every spring and fall had not arisen. Yet I was reckoned a well-appearing girl, who dressed liberally. Now, a young lady who has a waterfall-hat, an oriole-hat, and a jockey, must still be troubled with anxious cares for her spring and fall and summer and winter bonnets, — all the variety will not take the place of them. Gloves are bought by the dozen ; and as to dresses, there seems to be no limit to the quantity of material and trimming that may be expended upon them. When I was a young lady, seventy-five dollars a year was considered by careful parents a liberal allowance

for a daughter's wardrobe. I had a hundred, and was
reckoned rich ; and I sometimes used a part to make
up the deficiencies in the allowance of Sarah Evans,
my particular friend, whose father gave her only fifty.
We all thought that a very scant allowance ; yet she
generally made a very pretty and genteel appearance,
with the help of occasional presents from friends."

"How could a girl dress for fifty dollars?" said
Marianne.

"She could get a white muslin and a white cam-
bric, which, with different sortings of ribbons, served
her for all dress-occasions. A silk, in those days,
took only ten yards in the making, and one dark silk
was considered a reasonable allowance to a lady's
wardrobe. Once made, it stood for something, —
always worn carefully, it lasted for years. One or two
calico morning-dresses, and a merino for winter wear,
completed the list. Then, as to collars, capes, cuffs,
etc., we all did our own embroidering, and very pretty
things we wore, too. Girls looked as prettily then as
they do now, when four or five hundred dollars a year
is insufficient to clothe them."

"But, mamma, you know our allowance is n't anything like that, — it is quite a slender one, though not
so small as yours was," said Marianne. "Don't you
think the customs of society make a difference? Do
you think, as things are, we could go back and dress
for the sum you did?"

8

"You cannot," said my wife, "without a greater sacrifice of feeling than I wish to impose on you. Still, though I don't see how to help it, I cannot but think that the requirements of fashion are becoming needlessly extravagant, particularly in regard to the dress of women. It seems to me, it is making the support of families so burdensome that young men are discouraged from marriage. A young man, in a moderately good business, might cheerfully undertake the world with a wife who could make herself pretty and attractive for seventy-five dollars a year, when he might sigh in vain for one who positively could not get through, and be decent, on four hundred. Women, too, are getting to be so attached to the trappings and accessories of life, that they cannot think of marriage without an amount of fortune which few young men possess."

"You are talking in very low numbers about the dress of women," said Miss Featherstone. "I do assure you that it is the easiest thing in the world for a girl to make away with a thousand dollars a year, and not have so much to show for it either as Marianne and Jenny."

"To be sure," said I. "Only establish certain formulas of expectation, and it is the easiest thing in the world. For instance, in your mother's day girls talked of a pair of gloves, — now they talk of a pack; then

it was a bonnet summer and winter,—now it is a bonnet spring, summer, autumn, and winter, and hats like
monthly roses,—a new blossom every few weeks."

"And then," said my wife, "every device of the
toilet is immediately taken up and varied and improved on, so as to impose an almost monthly necessity for novelty.   The jackets of May are outshone by
the jackets of June; the buttons of June are antiquated in July; the trimmings of July are *passées* by
September; side-combs, back-combs, puffs, rats, and
all sorts of such matters, are in a distracted race of
improvement; every article of feminine toilet is on
the move towards perfection.   It seems to me that an
infinity of money must be spent in these trifles, by
those who make the least pretension to keep in the
fashion."

"Well, papa," said Jenny, "after all, it's just the
way things always have been since the world began.
You know the Bible says, 'Can a maid forget her
ornaments?'   It's clear she can't.   You see, it's a
law of Nature; and you remember all that long chapter in the Bible that we had read in church last Sunday, about the curls and veils and tinkling ornaments
and crimping-pins, and all that of those wicked daughters of Zion in old times.   Women always have been
too much given to dress, and they always will be."

"The thing is," said Marianne, "how can any

woman, I, for example, know what is too much or too little? In mamma's day, it seems, a girl could keep her place in society, by hard economy, and spend only fifty dollars a year on her dress. Mamma found a hundred dollars ample. I have more than that, and find myself quite straitened to keep myself looking well. I don't want to live for dress, to give all my time and thoughts to it; I don't wish to be extravagant; and yet I wish to be lady-like; it annoys and makes me unhappy not to be fresh and neat and nice; shabbiness and seediness are my aversion. I don't see where the fault is. Can one individual resist the whole current of society? It certainly is not strictly necessary for us girls to have half the things we do. We might, I suppose, live without many of them, and, as mamma says, look just as well, because girls did so before these things were invented. Now, I confess, I flatter myself, generally, that I am a pattern of good management and economy, because I get so much less than other girls I associate with. I wish you could see Miss Thorne's fall dresses that she showed me last year when she was visiting here. She had six gowns, and no one of them could have cost less than seventy or eighty dollars, and some of them must have been even more expensive; and yet I don't doubt that this fall she will feel that she must have just as many more. She runs through and wears out these expensive things, with all their velvet and thread lace, just as I wear my commonest ones; and at the end of the season they are really gone, — spotted, stained, frayed, the lace all pulled to pieces, — nothing left to save or make over. I feel as if Jenny and I were patterns of economy, when I see such things. I really don't know what economy is. What is it?"

"There is the same difficulty in my housekeeping," said my wife. "I think I am an economist. I mean to be one. All our expenses are on a modest scale, and yet I can see much that really is not strictly necessary; but if I compare myself with some of my neighbors, I feel as if I were hardly respectable. There is no subject on which all the world are censuring one another so much as this. Hardly any one but thinks her neighbors extravagant in some one or more particulars, and takes for granted that she herself is an economist."

"I'll venture to say," said I, "that there isn't a woman of my acquaintance that does not think she is an economist."

"Papa is turned against us women, like all the rest of them," said Jenny. "I wonder if it isn't just so with the men?"

"Yes," said Marianne, "it's the fashion to talk as if all the extravagance of the country was perpetrated by women. For my part, I think young men are just as extravagant. Look at the sums they spend for cigars and meerschaums,—an expense which has n't even the pretence of usefulness in any way ; it 's a purely selfish, nonsensical indulgence. When a girl spends money in making herself look pretty, she contributes something to the agreeableness of society ; but a man's cigars and pipes are neither ornamental nor useful."

"Then look at their dress," said Jenny ; "they are to the full as fussy and particular about it as girls ; they have as many fine, invisible points of fashion, and their fashions change quite as often ; and they have just as many knick-knacks, with their studs and their sleeve-buttons and waistcoat-buttons, their scarfs and scarf-pins, their watch-chains and seals and seal-rings, and nobody knows what. Then they often waste and throw away more than women, because they are not good judges of material, nor saving in what they buy, and have no knowledge of how things should be cared for, altered, or mended. If their cap is a little too tight, they cut the lining with a pen-knife, or slit holes in a new shirt-collar, because it does not exactly fit to their mind. For my part, I think men are naturally twice as wasteful as women. A pretty thing, to be sure, to have all the waste of the country laid to us !"

"You are right, child," said I; "women are by nature, as compared with men, the care-taking and saving part of creation, — the authors and conservators of economy. As a general rule, man earns and woman saves and applies. The wastefulness of woman is commonly the fault of man."

"I don't see into that," said Bob Stephens.

"In this way. Economy is the science of proportion. Whether a particular purchase is extravagant depends mainly on the income it is taken from. Suppose a woman has a hundred and fifty a year for her dress, and gives fifty dollars for a bonnet; she gives a third of her income; — it is a horrible extravagance, while for the woman whose income is ten thousand it may be no extravagance at all. The poor clergyman's wife, when she gives five dollars for a bonnet, may be giving as much, in proportion to her income, as the woman who gives fifty. Now the difficulty with the greater part of women is, that the men who make the money and hold it give them no kind of standard by which to measure their expenses. Most women and girls are in this matter entirely at sea, without chart or compass. They don't know in the least what they have to spend. Husbands and fathers often pride themselves about not saying a word on business-matters to their wives and daughters. They don't wish them to understand them, or to inquire into them, or to make remarks or suggestions concerning them. 'I want you to have everything that is suitable and proper,' says Jones to his wife, 'but don't be extravagant.'

"'But, my dear,' says Mrs. Jones, 'what is suitable and proper depends very much on our means; if you could allow me any specific sum for dress and house-keeping, I could tell better.'

"'Nonsense, Susan! I can't do that, — it's too much trouble. Get what you need, and avoid foolish extravagances; that's all I ask.'

"By and by Mrs. Jones's bills are sent in, in an evil hour, when Jones has heavy notes to meet, and then comes a domestic storm.

"'I shall just be ruined, Madam, if that's the way you are going on. I can't afford to dress you and the girls in the style you have set up; — look at this milliner's bill!'

"'I assure you,' says Mrs. Jones, 'we have n't got any more than the Stebbinses, — nor so much.'

"'Don't you know that the Stebbinses are worth five times as much as ever I was?'

"No, Mrs. Jones did not know it; — how should she, when her husband makes it a rule never to speak of his business to her, and she has not the remotest idea of his income?

"Thus multitudes of good conscientious women

and girls are extravagant from pure ignorance. The male provider allows bills to be run up in his name, and they have no earthly means of judging whether they are spending too much or too little, except the semi-annual hurricane which attends the coming in of these bills.

"The first essential in the practice of economy is a knowledge of one's income, and the man who refuses to accord to his wife and children this information has never any right to accuse them of extravagance, because he himself deprives them of that standard of comparison which is an indispensable requisite in economy. As early as possible in the education of children they should pass from that state of irresponsible waiting to be provided for by parents, and be trusted with the spending of some fixed allowance, that they may learn prices and values, and have some notion of what money is actually worth and what it will bring. The simple fact of the possession of a fixed and definite income often suddenly transforms a giddy, extravagant girl into a care-taking, prudent little woman. Her allowance is her own ; she begins to plan upon it, — to add, subtract, multiply, divide, and do numberless sums in her little head. She no longer buys everything she fancies ; she deliberates, weighs, compares. And now there is room for self-denial and generosity to come in. She can do with-

8*

out this article ; she can furbish up some older possession to do duty a little longer, and give this money
to some friend poorer than she ; and ten to one the
girl whose bills last year were four or five hundred
finds herself bringing through this year creditably on
a hundred and fifty.   To be sure, she goes without
numerous things which she used to have.   From the
stand-point of a fixed income she sees that these are
impossible, and no more wants them than the green
cheese of the moon.   She learns to make her own
taste and skill take the place of expensive purchases.
She refits her hats and bonnets, retrims her dresses,
and in a thousand busy, earnest, happy little ways, sets
herself to make the most of her small income.

"So the woman who has her definite allowance for
housekeeping finds at once a hundred questions set
at rest.   Before, it was not clear to her why she should
not 'go and do likewise' in relation to every purchase
made by her next neighbor.   Now, there is a clear
logic of proportion.   Certain things are evidently not
to be thought of, though next neighbors do have
them ; and we must resign ourselves to find some
other way of living."

"My dear," said my wife, "I think there is a peculiar temptation in a life organized as ours is in
America.   There are here no settled classes, with
similar ratios of income.   Mixed together in the

same society, going to the same parties, and blended in daily neighborly intercourse, are families of the most opposite extremes in point of fortune. In England there is a very well understood expression, that people should not dress or live above their station ; in America none will admit that they have any particular station, or that they can live above it. The principle of democratic equality unites in society people of the most diverse positions and means.

"Here, for instance, is a family like Dr. Selden's, an old and highly respected one, with an income of only two or three thousand, — yet they are people universally sought for in society, and mingle in all the intercourse of life with merchant-millionnaires whose incomes are from ten to thirty thousand. Their sons and daughters go to the same schools, the same parties, and are thus constantly meeting upon terms of social equality.

"Now it seems to me that our danger does not lie in the great and evident expenses of our richer friends. We do not expect to have pineries, graperies, equipages, horses, diamonds, — we say openly and of course that we do not. Still, our expenses are constantly increased by the proximity of these things, unless we understand ourselves better than most people do. We don't of course, expect to get a fifteen-hundred-dollar Cashmere, like Mrs. So-and-so, but we begin to look at hundred-dollar shawls and nibble about the hook. We don't expect sets of diamonds, but a diamond ring, a pair of solitaire diamond earrings, begins to be speculated about among the young people as among possibilities. We don't expect to carpet our house with Axminster and hang our windows with damask, but at least we must have Brussels and brocatelle, — it *would not do* not to. And so we go on getting hundreds of things that we don't need, that have no real value except that they soothe our self-love, — and for these inferior articles we pay a higher proportion of our income than our rich neighbor does for his better ones. Nothing is uglier than low-priced Cashmere shawls ; and yet a young man just entering business will spend an eighth of a year's income to put one on his wife, and when he has put it there it only serves as a constant source of disquiet, — for now that the door is opened, and Cashmere shawls are possible, she is consumed with envy at the superior ones constantly sported around her. So also with point-lace, velvet dresses, and hundreds of things of that sort, which belong to a certain rate of income, and are absurd below it."

"And yet, mamma, I heard Aunt Easygo say that velvet, point-lace, and Cashmere were the cheapest finery that could be bought, because they lasted a lifetime."

"Aunt Easygo speaks from an income of ten thousand a year; they may be cheap for her rate of living, — but for us, for example, by no magic of numbers can it be made to appear that it is cheaper to have the greatest bargain in the world in Cashmere, lace, and diamonds, than not to have them at all. I never had a diamond, never wore a piece of point-lace, never had a velvet dress, and have been perfectly happy, and just as much respected as if I had. Who ever thought of objecting to me for not having them? Nobody, as I ever heard."

"Certainly not, mamma," said Marianne.

"The thing I have always said to you girls is, that you were not to expect to live like richer people, not to begin to try, not to think or inquire about certain rates of expenditure, or take the first step in certain directions. We have moved on all our life after a very antiquated and old-fashioned mode. We have had our little old-fashioned house, our little old-fashioned ways."

"Except the parlor-carpet, and what came of it, my dear," said I, mischievously.

"Yes, except the parlor-carpet," said my wife, with a conscious twinkle, "and the things that came of it; there was a concession there, but one can't be wise always."

"*We* talked mamma into that," said Jenny.

" But one thing is certain," said my wife, — " that, though I have had an antiquated, plain house, and plain furniture, and plain dress, and not the beginning of a thing such as many of my neighbors have possessed, I have spent more money than many of them for real comforts. While I had young children, I kept more and better servants than many women who wore Cashmeres and diamonds. I thought it better to pay extra wages to a really good, trusty woman who lived with me from year to year, and relieved me of some of my heaviest family-cares, than to have ever so much lace locked away in my drawers. We always were able to go into the country to spend our summers, and to keep a good family-horse and carriage for daily driving, — by which means we afforded, as a family, very poor patronage to the medical profession. Then we built our house, and while we left out a great many expensive commonplaces that other people think they must have, we put in a profusion of bathing accommodations such as very few people think of having. There never was a time when we did not feel able to afford to do what was necessary to preserve or to restore health ; and for this I always drew on the surplus fund laid up by my very unfashionable housekeeping and dressing."

" Your mother has had," said I, " what is the great

want in America, perfect independence of mind to go
her own way without regard to the way others go. I
think there is, for some reason, more false shame
among Americans about economy than among Euro-
peans. 'I cannot afford it' is more seldom heard
among us. A young man beginning life, whose income may be from five to eight hundred a year,
thinks it elegant and gallant to affect a careless air
about money, especially among ladies, — to hand it
out freely, and put back his change without counting
it, — to wear a watch-chain and studs and shirt-fronts
like those of some young millionnaire. None but the
most expensive tailors, shoemakers, and hatters will
do for him ; and then he grumbles at the dearness of
living, and declares that he cannot get along on his
salary. The same is true of young girls, and of married men and women too, — the whole of them are
ashamed of economy. The cares that wear out life
and health in many households are of a nature that
cannot be cast on God, or met by any promise from
the Bible, — it is not care for 'food convenient,' or
for comfortable raiment, but care to keep up false appearances, and to stretch a narrow income over the
space that can be covered only by a wider one.

"The poor widow in her narrow lodgings, with her
monthly rent staring her hourly in the face, and her
bread and meat and candles and meal all to be paid

for on delivery or not obtained at all, may find comfort in the good old Book, reading of that other widow whose wasting measure of oil and last failing handful of meal were of such account before her Father in heaven that a prophet was sent to recruit them ; and when customers do not pay, or wages are cut down, she can enter into her chamber, and when she hath shut her door, present to her Father in heaven His sure promise that with the fowls of the air she shall be fed and with the lilies of the field she shall be clothed : but what promises are there for her who is racking her brains on the ways and means to provide as sumptuous an entertainment of oysters and Champagne at her next party as her richer neighbor, or to compass that great bargain which shall give her a point-lace set almost as handsome as that of Mrs. Crœsus, who has ten times her income?"

"But, papa," said Marianne, with a twinge of that exacting sensitiveness by which the child is characterized, "I think I am an economist, thanks to you and mamma, so far as knowing just what my income is, and keeping within it ; but that does not satisfy me, and it seems that is n't all of economy ; — the question that haunts me is, Might I not make my little all do more and better than I do?".

"There," said I, "you have hit the broader and deeper signification of economy, which is, in fact, the science of *comparative values*. In its highest sense, economy is a just judgment of the comparative value of things, — money only the means of enabling one to express that value. This is the reason why the whole matter is so full of difficulty, — why every one criticises his neighbor in this regard. Human beings are so various, the necessities of each are so different, they are made comfortable or uncomfortable by such opposite means, that the spending of other people's incomes must of necessity often look unwise from our stand-point. For this reason multitudes of people who cannot be accused of exceeding their incomes often seem to others to be spending them foolishly and extravagantly."

"But is there no standard of value?" said Marianne.

"There are certain things upon which there is a pretty general agreement, verbally, at least, among mankind. For instance, it is generally agreed that *health* is an indispensable good, — that money is well spent that secures it, and worse than ill spent that ruins it.

"With this standard in mind, how much money is wasted even by people who do not exceed their income! Here a man builds a house, and pays, in the first place, ten thousand more than he need, for a location in a fashionable part of the city, though the air will be closer and the chances of health less ; he spends three or four thousand more on a stone front, on marble mantles imported from Italy, on plate-glass windows, plated hinges, and a thousand nice points of finish, and has perhaps but one bath-room for a whole household, and that so connected with his own apartment that nobody but himself and his wife can use it.

"Another man buys a lot in an open, airy situation, which fashion has not made expensive, and builds without a stone front, marble mantels, or plate-glass windows, but has a perfect system of ventilation through his house, and bathing-rooms in every story, so that the children and guests may all, without inconvenience, enjoy the luxury of abundant water.

"The first spends for fashion and show, the second for health and comfort.

"Here is a man that will buy his wife a diamond bracelet and a lace shawl, and take her yearly to Washington to show off her beauty in ball-dresses, who yet will not let her pay wages which will command any but the poorest and most inefficient domestic service. The woman is worn out, her life made a desert by exhaustion consequent on a futile attempt to keep up a showy establishment with only half the hands needed for the purpose. Another family will give brilliant parties, have a gay season every year at the first hotels at Newport, and not be able to afford the wife a fire in her chamber in midwinter, or the servants enough food to keep them from constantly deserting. The damp, mouldy, dingy cellar-kitchen, the cold, windy, desolate attic, devoid of any comfort, where the domestics are doomed to pass their whole time, are witnesses to what such families consider economy. Economy in the view of some is undisguised slipshod slovenliness in the home-circle for the sake of fine clothes to be shown abroad; it is undisguised hard selfishness to servants and dependants, counting their every approach to comfort a needless waste, — grudging the Roman-Catholic cook her cup of tea at dinner on Friday, when she must not eat meat, — and murmuring that a cracked, second-hand looking-glass must be got for the servants' room : what business have they to want to know how they look ?

" Some families will employ the cheapest physician, without regard to his ability to kill or cure ; some will treat diseases in their incipiency with quack medicines, bought cheap, hoping thereby to fend off the doctor's bill. Some women seem to be pursued by an evil demon of economy, which, like an *ignis fatuus* in a bog, delights constantly to tumble them over into the mire of expense. They are dismayed at the quantity of sugar in the recipe for preserves, leave out a quarter, and the whole ferments and is spoiled. They cannot by any means be induced at any one time to buy enough silk to make a dress, and the dress finally, after many convulsions and alterations, must be thrown by altogether, as too scanty. They get poor needles, poor thread, poor sugar, poor raisins, poor tea, poor coal. One wonders, in looking at their blackened, smouldering grates, in a freezing day, what the fire is there at all for, — it certainly warms nobody. The only thing they seem likely to be lavish in is funeral expenses, which come in the wake of leaky shoes and imperfect clothing. These funeral expenses at last swallow all, since nobody can dispute an undertaker's bill. One pities these joyless beings. Economy, instead of a rational act of the judgment, is a morbid monomania, eating the pleasure out of life, and haunting them to the grave.

"Some people's ideas of economy seem to run simply in the line of eating. Their flour is of an extra brand, their meat the first cut ; the delicacies of every season, in their dearest stages, come home to their table with an apologetic smile, — 'It was scandalously dear, my love, but I thought we must just treat ourselves.' And yet these people cannot afford to buy books, and pictures they regard as an unthought-of extravagance. Trudging home with fifty dollars' worth of delicacies on his arm, Smith meets Jones,

who is exulting with a bag of crackers under one arm
and a choice little bit of an oil painting under the
other, which he thinks a bargain at fifty dollars. '*I*
can't afford to buy pictures,' Smith says to his spouse,
' and I don't know how Jones and his wife manage.'
Jones and his wife will live on bread and milk for a
month, and she will turn her best gown the third time,
but they will have their picture, and they are happy.
Jones's picture remains, and Smith's fifty dollars' worth
of oysters and canned fruit to-morrow will be gone
forever. Of all modes of spending money, the swal-
lowing of expensive dainties brings the least return.
There is one step lower than this, — the consuming
of luxuries that are injurious to the health. If all the
money spent on tobacco and liquors could be spent
in books and pictures, I predict that nobody's health
would be a whit less sound, and houses would be
vastly more attractive. There is enough money spent
in smoking, drinking, and over-eating to give every
family in the community a good library, to hang everybody's parlor-walls with lovely pictures, to set up in
every house a conservatory which should bloom all
winter with choice flowers, to furnish every dwelling
with ample bathing and warming accommodations,
even down to the dwellings of the poor ; and in the
millennium I believe this is the way things are to be.

" In these times of peril and suffering, if the inquiry

arises, How shall there be retrenchment? I answer,
First and foremost retrench things needless, doubtful,
and positively hurtful, as rum, tobacco, and all the
meerschaums of divers colors that do accompany the
same. Second, retrench all eating not necessary to
health and comfort. A French family would live in
luxury on the leavings that are constantly coming from
the tables of those who call themselves in middling
circumstances. There are superstitions of the table
that ought to be broken through. Why must you
always have cake in your closet? why need you feel
undone to entertain a guest with no cake on your tea-
table? Do without it a year, and ask yourselves if
you or your children, or any one else, have suffered
materially in consequence.

"Why is it imperative that you should have two or
three courses at every meal? Try the experiment of
having but one, and that a very good one, and see if
any great amount of suffering ensues. Why must
social intercourse so largely consist in eating? In
Paris there is a very pretty custom. Each family has
one evening in the week when it stays at home and
receives friends. Tea, with a little bread and butter
and cake, served in the most informal way, is the
only refreshment. The rooms are full, busy, bright,
— everything as easy and joyous as if a monstrous
supper, with piles of jelly and mountains of cake,

were waiting to give the company a nightmare at the close.

"Said a lady, pointing to a gentleman and his wife in a social circle of this kind, 'I ought to know them well,—I have seen them every week for twenty years.' It is certainly pleasant and confirmative of social enjoyment for friends to eat together; but a little enjoyed in this way answers the purpose as well as a great deal, and better too."

"Well, papa," said Marianne, "in the matter of dress now,—how much ought one to spend just to look as others do?"

"I will tell you what I saw the other night, girls, in the parlor of one of our hotels. Two middle-aged Quaker ladies came gliding in, with calm, cheerful faces, and lustrous dove-colored silks. By their conversation I found that they belonged to that class of women among the Friends who devote themselves to travelling on missions of benevolence. They had just completed a tour of all the hospitals for wounded soldiers in the country, where they had been carrying comforts, arranging, advising, and soothing by their cheerful, gentle presence. They were now engaged on another mission, to the lost and erring of their own sex; night after night, guarded by a policeman, they had ventured after midnight into the dance-houses where girls are being led to ruin, and with gentle

words of tender, motherly counsel sought to win them
from their fatal ways,—telling them where they might
go the next day to find friends who would open to
them an asylum and aid them to seek a better life.

"As I looked upon these women, dressed with such
modest purity, I began secretly to think that the
Apostle was not wrong, when he spoke of women
adorning themselves with the *ornament* of a meek
and quiet spirit ; for the habitual gentleness of their
expression, the calmness and purity of the lines in
their faces, the delicacy and simplicity of their apparel,
seemed of themselves a rare and peculiar beauty.
I could not help thinking that fashionable bonnets,
flowing lace sleeves, and dresses elaborately trimmed
could not have improved even their outward appearance. Doubtless, their simple wardrobe needed but
a small trunk in travelling from place to place, and
hindered but little their prayers and ministrations.

" Now, it is true, all women are not called to such
a life as this ; but might not all women take a leaf at
least from their book ? I submit the inquiry humbly.
It seems to me that there are many who go monthly
to the sacrament, and receive it with sincere devotion,
and who give thanks each time sincerely that they are
thus made 'members incorporate in the mystical body
of Christ,' who have never thought of this membership
as meaning that they should share Christ's sacrifices

for lost souls, or abridge themselves of one ornament or encounter one inconvenience for the sake of those wandering sheep for whom he died. Certainly there is a higher economy which we need to learn, — that which makes all things subservient to the spiritual and immortal, and that not merely to the good of our own souls and those of our family, but of all who are knit with us in the great bonds of human brotherhood.

"There have been from time to time, among well-meaning Christian people, retrenchment societies on high moral grounds, which have failed for want of knowledge how to manage the complicated question of necessaries and luxuries. These words have a signification in the case of different people as varied as the varieties of human habit and constitution. It is a department impossible to be bound by external rules ; but none the less should every high-minded Christian soul in this matter have a law unto itself. It may safely be laid down as a general rule, that no income, however large or however small, should be unblessed by the divine touch of self-sacrifice. Something for the poor, the sorrowing, the hungry, the tempted, and the weak should be taken from *what is our own* at the expense of some personal sacrifice, or we suffer more morally than the brother from whom we withdraw it. Even the Lord of all, when dwelling among men, out of that slender private purse which he accepted for

9

his little family of chosen ones, had ever something reserved to give to the poor. It is easy to say, ' It is but a drop in the bucket. I cannot remove the great mass of misery in the world. What little I could save or give does nothing.' It does this, if no more, — it prevents one soul, and that soul your own, from drying and hardening into utter selfishness and insensibility; it enables you to say I have done something; taken one atom from the great heap of sins and miseries and placed it on the side of good.

" The Sisters of Charity and the Friends, each with their different costume of plainness and self-denial, and other noble-hearted women of no particular outward order, but kindred in spirit, have shown to womanhood, on the battle-field and in the hospital, a more excellent way, — a beauty and nobility before which all the common graces and ornaments of the sex fade, appear like dim candles by the pure, eternal stars."

IX.

SERVANTS.

IN the course of my papers various domestic revo-
lutions have occurred. Our Marianne has gone
from us with a new name to a new life, and a modest
little establishment not many squares off claims about
as much of my wife's and Jenny's busy thoughts as
those of the proper mistress.

Marianne, as I always foresaw, is a careful and
somewhat anxious housekeeper. Her tastes are fastidious ; she is made for exactitude : the smallest
departures from the straight line appear to her shocking deviations. She had always lived in a house
where everything had been formed to quiet and order
under the ever-present care and touch of her mother ;
nor had she ever participated in these cares more than
to do a little dusting of the parlor ornaments, or wash
the best china, or make sponge-cake or chocolate-
caramels. Certain conditions of life had always appeared so to be matters of course that she had never
conceived of a house without them. It never occurred
to her that such bread and biscuit as she saw at the

home-table would not always and of course appear at every table, — that the silver would not always be as bright, the glass as clear, the salt as fine and smooth, the plates and dishes as nicely arranged as she had always seen them, apparently without the thought or care of any one, — for my wife is one of those house-keepers whose touch is so fine that no one feels it. She is never heard scolding or reproving, — never entertains her company with her recipes for cookery or the faults of her servants.   She is so unconcerned about receiving her own personal share of credit for the good appearance of her establishment, that even the children of the house have not supposed that there is any particular will of hers in the matter, — it all seems the natural consequence of having very good servants.

One phenomenon they had never seriously reflected on, — that, under all the changes of the domestic cabinet which are so apt to occur in American households, the same coffee, the same bread and biscuit, the same nicely prepared dishes and neatly laid table always gladdened their eyes ; and from this they inferred only that good servants were more abundant than most people had supposed.   They were somewhat surprised when these marvels were wrought by professedly green hands, but were given to suppose that these green hands must have had some remarkable quickness or aptitude for acquiring. That sparkling jelly, well-flavored ice-creams, clear soups, and delicate biscuits could be made by a raw Irish girl, fresh from her native Erin, seemed to them a proof of the genius of the race ; and my wife, who never felt it important to attain to the reputation of a cook, quietly let it pass.

For some time, therefore, after the inauguration of the new household, there was trouble in the camp. Sour bread had appeared on the table, — bitter, acrid coffee had shocked and astonished the palate, — lint had been observed on tumblers, and the spoons had sometimes dingy streaks on the brightness of their first bridal polish, — beds were detected made shockingly awry, — and Marianne came burning with indignation to her mother.

"Such a little family as we have, and two strong girls," said she, — "everything ought to be perfect ; there is really nothing to do. Think of a whole batch of bread absolutely sour ! and when I gave that away, then this morning another exactly like it ! and when I talked to cook about it, she said she had lived in this and that family, and her bread had always been praised as equal to the baker's ! "

"I don't doubt she is right," said I. "Many families never have anything but sour bread from one end of the year to the other, eating it unperceiving, and with good cheer ; and they buy also sour bread of the baker, with like approbation, — lightness being in their estimation the only virtue necessary in the article."

"Could you not correct her fault?" suggested my wife.

"I have done all I can. I told her we could not have such bread, that it was dreadful; Bob says it would give him the dyspepsia in a week; and then she went and made exactly the same; — it seems to me mere wilfulness."

"But," said I, "suppose, instead of such general directions, you should analyze her proceedings and find out just where she makes her mistake, — is the root of the trouble in the yeast, or in the time she begins it, letting it rise too long? — the time, you know, should vary so much with the temperature of the weather."

"As to that," said Marianne, "I know nothing. I never noticed; it never was my business to make bread; it always seemed quite a simple process, mixing yeast and flour and kneading it; and our bread at home was always good."

"It seems, then, my dear, that you have come to your profession without even having studied it."

My wife smiled, and said, —

"You know, Marianne, I proposed to you to be our family bread-maker for one month of the year before you married."

"Yes, mamma, I remember; but I was like other girls; I thought there was no need of it. I never liked to do such things; perhaps I had better have done it."

"You certainly had," said I; "for the first business of a housekeeper in America is that of a teacher. She can have a good table only by having practical knowledge, and tact in imparting it. If she understands her business practically and experimentally, her eye detects at once the weak spot; it requires only a little tact, some patience, some clearness in giving directions, and all comes right. I venture to say that your mother would have exactly such bread as always appears on our table, and have it by the hands of your cook, because she could detect and explain to her exactly her error."

"Do you know," said my wife, "what yeast she uses?"

"I believe," said Marianne, "it's a kind she makes herself. I think I heard her say so. I know she makes a great fuss about it, and rather values herself upon it. She is evidently accustomed to being praised for her bread, and feels mortified and angry, and I don't know how to manage her."

"Well," said I, "if you carry your watch to a watchmaker, and undertake to show him how to regulate the machinery, he laughs and goes on his own way; but if a brother-machinist makes suggestions, he listens respectfully. So, when a woman who knows nothing of woman's work undertakes to instruct one who knows more than she does, she makes no impression; but a woman who has been trained experimentally, and shows she understands the matter thoroughly, is listened to with respect."

"I think," said my wife, "that your Bridget is worth teaching. She is honest, well-principled, and tidy. She has good recommendations from excellent families, whose ideas of good bread it appears differ from ours; and with a little good-nature, tact, and patience, she will come into your ways."

"But the coffee, mamma, — you would not imagine it to be from the same bag with your own, so dark and so bitter; what do you suppose she has done to it?"

"Simply this," said my wife. "She has let the berries stay a few moments too long over the fire, — they are burnt, instead of being roasted; and there are people who think it essential to good coffee that it should look black, and have a strong, bitter flavor. A very little change in the preparing will alter this."

"Now," said I, "Marianne, if you want my advice, I'll give it to you gratis: — Make your own bread for one month. Simple as the process seems, I think it will take as long as that to give you a thorough knowledge of all the possibilities in the case; but after that you will never need to make any more, — you will be able to command good bread by the aid of all sorts of servants; you will, in other words, be a thoroughly prepared teacher."

"I did not think," said Marianne, "that so simple a thing required so much attention."

"It is simple," said my wife, "and yet requires a delicate care and watchfulness. There are fifty ways to spoil good bread; there are a hundred little things to be considered and allowed for that require accurate observation and experience. The same process that will raise good bread in cold weather will make sour bread in the heat of summer; different qualities of flour require variations in treatment, as also different sorts and conditions of yeast; and when all is done, the baking presents another series of possibilities which require exact attention."

"So it appears," said Marianne, gayly, "that I must begin to study my profession at the eleventh hour."

"Better late than never," said I. "But there is this advantage on your side: a well-trained mind, accustomed to reflect, analyze, and generalize, has an advantage over uncultured minds even of double experience. Poor as your cook is, she now knows more of her business than you do. After a very brief period of attention and experiment, you will not only

9*

know more than she does, but you will convince her
that you do, which is quite as much to the purpose."

" In the same manner," said my wife, " you will
have to give lessons to your other girl on the washing
of silver and the making of beds.   Good servants do
not often come to us ; they must be *made* by patience
and training ; and if a girl has a good disposition and
a reasonable degree of handiness, and the housekeeper understands her profession, she may make a
good servant out of an indifferent one.   Some of my
best girls have been those who came to me directly
from the ship, with no preparation but docility and
some natural quickness.   The hardest cases to be
managed are not of those who have been taught nothing, but of those who have been taught wrongly, —
who come to you self-opinionated, with ways which
are distasteful to you, and contrary to the genius of
your housekeeping.   Such require that their mistress
shall understand at least so much of the actual conduct of affairs as to prove to the servant that there are
better ways than those in which she has hitherto been
trained."

" Don't you think, mamma," said Marianne, " that
there has been a sort of reaction against woman's
work in our day? So much has been said of the
higher sphere of woman, and so much has been done
to find some better work for her, that insensibly, I

think, almost everybody begins to feel that it is rather!
degrading for a woman in good society to be much
tied down to family affairs.")

" Especially," said my wife, " since in these Woman's-Rights Conventions there is so much indignation expressed at those who would confine her ideas
to the kitchen and nursery."

" There is reason in all things," said I. "Woman's-
Rights Conventions are a protest against many former
absurd, unreasonable ideas, — the mere physical and
culinary idea of womanhood as connected only with
puddings and shirt-buttons, the unjust and unequal
burdens which the laws of harsher ages had cast upon
the sex. Many of the women connected with these
movements are as superior in everything properly
womanly as they are in exceptional talent and culture. There is no manner of doubt that the sphere
of woman is properly to be enlarged, and that republican governments in particular are to be saved
from corruption and failure only by allowing to woman
this enlarged sphere. Every woman has rights as a
human being first, which belong to no sex, and
ought to be as freely conceded to her as if she were
a man, — and first and foremost, the great right of
doing anything which God and Nature evidently have
fitted her to excel in. If she be made a natural
orator, like Miss Dickenson, or an astronomer, like

Mrs. Somerville, or a singer, like Grisi, let not the technical rules of womanhood be thrown in the way of her free use of her powers. Nor can there be any reason shown why a woman's vote in the state should not be received with as much respect as in the family. A state is but an association of families, and laws relate to the rights and immunities which touch woman's most private and immediate wants and dearest hopes ; and there is no reason why sister, wife, and mother should be more powerless in the state than in the home: Nor does it make a woman unwomanly to express an opinion by dropping a slip of paper into a box, more than to express that same opinion by conversation. In fact, there is no doubt, that, in all matters relating to the interests of education, temperance, and religion, the state would be a material gainer by receiving the votes of women.

" But, having said all this, I must admit, *per contra*, not only a great deal of crude, disagreeable talk in these conventions, but a too great tendency of the age to make the education of women anti-domestic. It seems as if the world never could advance, except like ships under a head-wind, tacking and going too far, now in this direction, and now in the opposite. Our common-school system now rejects sewing from the education of girls, which very properly used to occupy many hours daily in school a generation ago. The daughters of laborers and artisans are put through algebra, geometry, trigonometry, and the higher mathematics, to the entire neglect of that learning which belongs distinctively to woman. A girl cannot keep pace with her class, if she gives any time to domestic matters; and accordingly she is excused from them all during the whole term of her education. The boy of a family, at an early age, is put to a trade, or the labors of a farm; the father becomes impatient of his support, and requires of him to care for himself. Hence an interrupted education, — learning coming by snatches in the winter months or in the intervals of work. As the result, the females in our country towns are commonly, in mental culture, vastly in advance of the males of the same household; but with this comes a physical delicacy, the result of an exclusive use of the brain and a neglect of the muscular system, with great inefficiency in practical domestic duties. The race of strong, hardy, cheerful girls, that used to grow up in country places, and made the bright, neat, New England kitchens of old times, — the girls that could wash, iron, brew, bake, harness a horse and drive him, no less than braid straw, embroider, draw, paint, and read innumerable books, — this race of women, pride of olden time, is daily lessening; and in their stead come the fragile, easily fatigued, languid girls of a modern age, drilled in book-learning, ignorant of common things. The great danger of all this, and of the evils that come from it, is that society by and by will turn as blindly against female intellectual culture as it now advocates it, and, having worked disproportionately one way, will work disproportionately in the opposite direction."

" The fact is," said my wife, "that domestic service is the great problem of life here in America; the happiness of families, their thrift, well-being, and comfort, are more affected by this than by any one thing else. Our girls, as they have been brought up, cannot perform the labor of their own families, as in those simpler, old-fashioned days you tell of; and what is worse, they have no practical skill with which to instruct servants, and servants come to us, as a class, raw and untrained; so what is to be done? In the present state of prices, the board of a domestic costs double her wages, and the waste she makes is a more serious matter still. Suppose you give us an article upon this subject in your 'House and Home Papers.' You could not have a better one."

So I sat down, and wrote thus on

Servants and Service.

MANY of the domestic evils in America originate in the fact, that, while society here is· professedly based on new principles which ought to make social life in every respect different from the life of the Old World, yet these principles have never been so thought out and applied as to give consistency and harmony to our daily relations. America starts with a political organization based on a declaration of the primitive freedom and equality of all men. Every human being, according to this principle, stands on the same natural level with every other, and has the same chance to rise according to the degree of power or capacity given by the Creator. All our civil institutions are designed to preserve this equality, as far as possible, from generation to generation : there is no entailed property, there are no hereditary titles, no monopolies, no privileged classes, — all are to be as free to rise and fall as the waves of the sea.

The condition of domestic service, however, still retains about it something of the influences from feudal times, and from the near presence of slavery in neighboring States. All English literature, all the literature of the world, describes domestic service in the old feudal spirit and with the old feudal language, which regarded the master as belonging to a privileged class and the servant to an inferior one. There is not a play, not a poem, not a novel, not a history, that does not present this view. The master's rights, like the rights of kings, were supposed to rest in his being born in a superior rank. The good servant was one who, from childhood, had learned "to order himself lowly and reverently to all his betters." When New England brought to these shores the theory of democracy, she brought, in the persons of the first pilgrims, the habits of thought and of action formed in aristocratic communities. Winthrop's Journal, and all the old records of the earlier colonists, show households where masters and mistresses stood on the "right divine" of the privileged classes, howsoever they might have risen up against authorities themselves.

The first consequence of this state of things was a universal rejection of domestic service in all classes of American-born society. For a generation or two, there was, indeed, a sort of interchange of family strength, — sons and daughters engaging in the service of neighboring families, in default of a sufficient working-force of their own, but always on conditions of strict equality. The assistant was to share the table, the family sitting-room, and every honor and attention that might be claimed by son or daughter. When families increased in refinement and education so as to make these conditions of close intimacy with more uncultured neighbors disagreeable, they had to choose between such intimacies and the performance of their own domestic toil. No wages could induce a son or daughter of New England to take the condition of a servant on terms which they thought applicable to that of a slave. The slightest hint of a separate table was resented as an insult; not to enter the front-door, and not to sit in the front-parlor on state-occasions, was bitterly commented on as a personal indignity.

The well-taught, self-respecting daughters of farmers, the class most valuable in domestic service, gradually retired from it. They preferred any other employment, however laborious. Beyond all doubt, the labors of a well-regulated family are more healthy, more cheerful, more interesting, because less monotonous, than the mechanical toils of a factory; yet the girls of New England, with one consent, preferred the factory, and left the whole business of domestic service to a foreign population ; and they did it mainly because they would not take positions in families as an inferior laboring-class by the side of others of their own age who assumed as their prerogative to live without labor.

"I can't let you have one of my daughters," said an energetic matron to her neighbor from the city, who was seeking for a servant in her summer vacation ; "if you had n't daughters of your own, maybe I would ; but my girls ain't going to work so that your girls may live in idleness."

It was vain to offer money. " We don't need your money, ma'am, we can support ourselves in other ways ; my girls can braid straw, and bind shoes, but they ain't going to be slaves to anybody."

In the Irish and German servants who took the place of Americans in families, there was, to begin with, the tradition of education in favor of a higher class ; but even the foreign population became more or less infected with the spirit of democracy. They came to this country with vague notions of freedom and equality, and in ignorant and uncultivated people such ideas are often more unreasonable for being vague. They did not, indeed, claim a seat at the table and in the parlor, but they repudiated many of those habits of respect and courtesy which belonged to their former condition, and asserted their own will and way in the round, unvàrnished phrase which they supposed to be their right as republican citizens. Life became a sort of domestic wrangle and struggle between the employers, who secretly confessed their weakness, but endeavored openly to assume the air and bearing of authority, and the employed, who knew their power and insisted on their privileges. From this cause domestic service in America has had less of mutual kindliness than in old countries. Its terms have been so ill understood and defined that both parties have assumed the defensive ; and a common topic of conversation in American female society has often been the general servile war which in one form or another was going on in their different families, — a war as interminable as would be a struggle between aristocracy and common people, undefined by any bill of rights or constitution, and therefore opening fields for endless disputes. In England, the class who go to service *are* a class, and service is a profession ; the distance between them and their employers is so marked and defined, and all the customs and requirements of the position are so perfectly understood, that the master or mistress has no fear of being compromised by condescension, and no need of the external voice or air of authority. The higher up in the social scale one goes, the more courteous seems to become the intercourse of master and servant ; the more perfect and real the power, the more is it veiled in outward expression, — commands are phrased as requests, and gentleness of voice and manner covers an authority which no one would think of offending without trembling.

But in America all is undefined. In the first place, there is no class who mean to make domestic service a profession to live and die in. It is universally an expedient, a stepping-stone to something higher ; your best servants always have something else in view as soon as they have laid by a little money ; some form of independence which shall give them a home of their own is constantly in mind. Families look forward to the buying of landed homesteads, and the scattered brothers and sisters work awhile in domestic service to gain the common fund for the purpose ; your seam-stress intends to become a dress-maker, and take in work at her own house ; your cook is pondering a marriage with the baker, which shall transfer her toils from your cooking-stove to her own. Young women are eagerly rushing into every other employment, till female trades and callings are all overstocked. We are continually harrowed with tales of the sufferings of distressed needle-women, of the exactions and ex-tortions practised on the frail sex in the many branches of labor and trade at which they try their hands ; and yet women will encounter all these chances of ruin and starvation rather than make up their minds to permanent domestic service. Now what is the mat-ter with domestic service ? One would think, on the face of it, that a calling which gives a settled home, a comfortable room, rent-free, with fire and lights, good board and lodging, and steady, well-paid wages, would certainly offer more attractions than the making of shirts for tenpence, with all the risks of providing one's own sustenance and shelter.

I think it is mainly from the want of a definite idea of the true position of a servant under our democratic institutions that domestic service is so shunned and avoided in America, that it is the very last thing which an intelligent young woman will look to for a living. It is more the want of personal respect toward those in that position than the labors incident to it which repels our people from it. Many would be willing to perform these labors, but they are not willing to place themselves in a situation where their self-respect is hourly wounded by *the implication of a degree of inferiority which does not follow any kind of labor or service in this country but that of the family.*

There exists in the minds of employers an unsuspected spirit of superiority, which is stimulated into an active form by the resistance which democracy inspires in the working-class. Many families think of servants only as a necessary evil, their wages as exactions, and all that is allowed them as so much taken from the family ; and they seek in every way to get from them as much and to give them as little as possible. Their rooms are the neglected, ill-furnished, incommodious ones, — and the kitchen is the most cheerless and comfortless place in the house. Other families, more good-natured and liberal, provide their domestics with more suitable accommodations, and are more indulgent ; but there is still a latent spirit of something like contempt for the position. That they treat their servants with so much consideration seems to them a merit entitling them to the most prostrate gratitude ; and they are constantly disappointed and shocked at that want of sense of inferiority on the part of these people which leads them to appropriate pleasant rooms, good furniture, and good living as mere matters of common justice.

It seems to be a constant surprise to some employers that servants should insist on having the same human wants as themselves. Ladies who yawn in their elegantly furnished parlors, among books and pictures, if they have not company, parties, or opera to diversify the evening, seem astonished and half indignant that cook and chambermaid are more disposed to go out for an evening gossip than to sit on hard chairs in the kitchen where they have been toiling all day. The pretty chambermaid's anxieties about her dress, the time she spends at her small and not very clear mirror, are sneeringly noticed by those whose toilet-cares take up serious hours ; and the question has never apparently occurred to them why a serving-maid should not want to look pretty as well as her mistress. She is a woman as well as they, with all a woman's wants and weaknesses ; and her dress is as much to her as theirs to them.

A vast deal of trouble among servants arises from impertinent interferences and petty tyrannical exactions on the part of employers. Now the authority of

the master and mistress of a house in regard to their
domestics extends simply to the things they have contracted to do and the hours during which they have
contracted to serve ; otherwise than this, they have no
more right to interfere with them in the disposal of
their time than with any mechanic whom they employ.
They have, indeed, a right to regulate the hours of
their own household, and servants can choose between conformity to these hours and the loss of their
situation ; but, within reasonable limits, their right to
come and go at their own discretion, in their own time,
should be unquestioned.

If employers are troubled by the fondness of their
servants for dancing, evening company, and late hours,
the proper mode of proceeding is to make these matters a subject of distinct contract in hiring. The more
strictly and perfectly the business matters of the first
engagement of domestics are conducted, the more
likelihood there is of mutual quiet and satisfaction in
the relation. It is quite competent to every housekeeper to say what practices are or are not consistent
with the rules of her family, and what will be incon-
sistent with the service for which she agrees to pay.
It is much better to regulate such affairs by cool contract in the outset than by warm altercations and
protracted domestic battles.

As to the terms of social intercourse, it seems some-

how to be settled in the minds of many employers
that their servants owe them and their family more
respect than they and the family owe to the servants.
But do they? What is the relation of servant to employer in a democratic country? Precisely that of a
person who for money performs any kind of service
for you. The carpenter comes into your house to
put up a set of shelves, — the cook comes into your
kitchen to cook your dinner. You never think that
the carpenter owes you any more respect than you
owe to him because he is in your house doing your
behests ; he is your fellow-citizen, you treat him with
respect, you expect to be treated with respect by him.
You have a claim on him that he shall do your work
according to your directions, — no more. Now I apprehend that there is a very common notion as to the
position and rights of servants which is quite different
from this. Is it not a common feeling that a servant
is one who may be treated with a degree of freedom
by every member of the family which he or she may
not return? Do not people feel at liberty to question
servants about their private affairs, to comment on
their dress and appearance, in a manner which they
would feel to be an impertinence, if reciprocated?
Do they not feel at liberty to express dissatisfaction
with their performances in rude and unceremonious
terms, to reprove them in the presence of company,

while yet they require that the dissatisfaction of servants shall be expressed only in terms of respect? A woman would not feel herself at liberty to talk to her milliner or her dressmaker in language as devoid of consideration as she will employ towards her cook or chambermaid. Yet both are rendering her a service which she pays for in money, and one is no more made her inferior thereby than the other. Both have an equal right to be treated with courtesy. The master and mistress of a house have a right to require respectful treatment from all whom their roof shelters; but they have no more right to exact it of servants than of every guest and every child, and they themselves owe it as much to servants as to guests.

In order that servants may be treated with respect and courtesy, it is not necessary, as in simpler patriarchal days, that they sit at the family-table. Your carpenter or plumber does not feel hurt that you do not ask him to dine with you, nor your milliner and mantua-maker that you do not exchange ceremonious calls and invite them to your parties. It is well understood that your relations with them are of a mere business character. They never take it as an assumption of superiority on your part that you do not admit them to relations of private intimacy. There may be the most perfect respect and esteem and even friendship between them and you, notwithstanding. So it

10

may be in the case of servants. It is easy to make any person understand that there are quite other reasons than the assumption of personal superiority for not wishing to admit servants to the family privacy. It was not, in fact, to sit in the parlor or at the table, in themselves considered, that was the thing aimed at by New England girls, — these were valued only as signs that they were deemed worthy of respect and consideration, and, where freely conceded, were often in point of fact declined.

Let servants feel, in their treatment by their employers, and in the atmosphere of the family, that their position is held to be a respectable one, let them feel in the mistress of the family the charm of unvarying consideration and good manners, let their work-rooms be made convenient and comfortable, and their private apartments bear some reasonable comparison in point of agreeableness to those of other members of the family, and domestic service will be more frequently sought by a superior and self-respecting class. There are families in which such a state of things prevails ; and such families, amid the many causes which unite to make the tenure of service uncertain, have generally been able to keep good permanent servants.

There is an extreme into which kindly disposed people often run with regard to servants, which may be mentioned here. They make pets of them. They give extravagant wages and indiscreet indulgences, and, through indolence and easiness of temper, tolerate neglect of duty. Many of the complaints of the ingratitude of servants come from those who have spoiled them in this way; while many of the longest and most harmonious domestic unions have sprung from a simple, quiet course of Christian justice and benevolence, a recognition of servants as fellow-beings and fellow-Christians, and a doing to them as we would in like circumstances that they should do to us.

The mistresses of American families, whether they like it or not, have the duties of missionaries imposed upon them by that class from which our supply of domestic servants is drawn. They may as well accept the position cheerfully, and, as one raw, untrained hand after another passes through their family, and is instructed by them in the mysteries of good housekeeping, comfort themselves with the reflection that they are doing something to form good wives and mothers for the Republic.

The complaints made of Irish girls are numerous and loud; the failings of green Erin, alas! are but too open and manifest; yet, in arrest of judgment, let us move this consideration: let us imagine our own daughters between the ages of sixteen and twenty-four, untaught and inexperienced in domestic affairs as they commonly are, shipped to a foreign shore to seek service in families. It may be questioned whether as a whole they would do much better. The girls that fill our families and do our house-work are often of the age of our own daughters, standing for themselves, without mothers to guide them, in a foreign country, not only bravely supporting themselves, but sending home in every ship remittances to impoverished friends left behind. If our daughters did as much for us, should we not be proud of their energy and heroism ?

When we go into the houses of our country, we find a majority of well-kept, well-ordered, and even elegant establishments where the only hands employed are those of the daughters of Erin. True, American women have been their instructors, and many a weary hour of care have they had in the discharge of this office ; but the result on the whole is beautiful and good, and the end of it, doubtless, will be peace.

In speaking of the office of the American mistress as being a missionary one, we are far from recommending any controversial interference with the religious faith of our servants. It is far better to incite them to be good Christians in their own way than to run the risk of shaking their faith in all religion by pointing out to them the errors of that in which they have been educated. The general purity of life and propriety of demeanor of so many thousands of undefended young girls cast yearly upon our shores, with no home but their church, and no shield but their religion, are a sufficient proof that this religion exerts an influence over them not to be lightly trifled with. But there is a real unity even in opposite Christian forms ; and the Roman Catholic servant and the Protestant mistress, if alike possessed by the spirit of Christ, and striving to conform to the Golden Rule, cannot help being one in heart, though one go to mass and the other to meeting.

Finally, the bitter baptism through which we are passing, the life-blood dearer than our own which is drenching distant fields, should remind us of the preciousness of distinctive American ideas. They who would seek in their foolish pride to establish the pomp of liveried servants in America are doing that which is simply absurd. A servant can never in our country be the mere appendage to another man, to be marked like a sheep with the color of his owner ; he must be a fellow-citizen, with an established position of his own, free to make contracts, free to come and go, and having in his sphere titles to consideration and respect just as definite as those of any trade or profession whatever.

Moreover, we cannot in this country maintain to any great extent large retinues of servants. Even with ample fortunes they are forbidden by the general character of society here, which makes them cumbrous and difficult to manage. Every mistress of a family knows that her cares increase with every additional servant. Two keep the peace with each other and their employer; three begin a possible discord, which possibility increases with four, and becomes certain with five or six. Trained housekeepers, such as regulate the complicated establishments of the Old World, form a class that are not, and from the nature of the case never will be, found in any great numbers in this country. All such women, as a general thing, are keeping, and prefer to keep, houses of their own.

A moderate style of housekeeping, small, compact, and simple domestic establishments, must necessarily be the general order of life in America. So many openings of profit are to be found in this country, that domestic service necessarily wants the permanence which forms so agreeable a feature of it in the Old World.

This being the case, it should be an object in America to exclude from the labors of the family all that can, with greater advantage, be executed out of it by combined labor.

Formerly, in New England, soap and candles were to be made in each separate family; now, comparatively few take this toil upon them. We buy soap of the soap-maker, and candles of the candle-factor. This principle might be extended much further. In France no family makes its own bread, and better bread cannot be eaten than what can be bought at the appropriate shops. No family does its own washing, the family's linen is all sent to women who, making this their sole profession, get it up with a care and nicety which can seldom be equalled in any family.

How would it simplify the burdens of the American housekeeper to have washing and ironing day expunged from her calendar! How much more neatly and compactly could the whole domestic system be arranged! If all the money that each separate family spends on the outfit and accommodations for washing and ironing, on fuel, soap, starch, and the other et ceteras, were united in a fund to create a laundry for every dozen families, one or two good women could do in first rate style what now is very indifferently done by the disturbance and disarrangement of all other domestic processes in these families. Whoever sets neighborhood laundries on foot will do much to solve the American housekeeper's hardest problem.

Finally, American ·women must not try with three servants to carry on life in the style which in the Old World requires sixteen, — they must thoroughly understand, and be prepared *to teach*, every branch of housekeeping, — they must study to make domestic service desirable, by treating their servants in a way to lead them to respect themselves and to feel themselves respected, — and there will gradually be evolved from the present confusion a solution of the domestic problem which shall be adapted to the life of a new and growing world.

X.

COOKERY.

MY wife and I were sitting at the open bow-window of my study, watching the tuft of bright red leaves on our favorite maple, which warned us that summer was over. I was solacing myself, like all the world in our days, with reading the "Schönberg Cotta Family," when my wife made her voice heard through the enchanted distance, and dispersed the pretty vision of German cotfage-life.

"Chris!"

"Well, my dear."

"Do you know the day of the month?"

Now my wife knows this is a thing that I never do know, that I can't know, and, in fact, that there is no need I should trouble myself about, since she always knows, and what is more, always tells me. In fact, the question, when asked by her, meant more than met the ear. It was a delicate way of admonishing me that another paper for the "Atlantic" ought to be in train; and so I answered, not to the external form, but to the internal intention.

10*

"Well, you see, my dear, I have n't made up my mind what my next paper shall be about."

"Suppose, then, you let me give you a subject."

"Sovereign lady, speak on! Your slave hears!"

"Well, then, take *Cookery*. It may seem a vulgar subject, but I think more of health and happiness depends on that than on any other one thing. You may make houses enchantingly beautiful, hang them with pictures, have them clean and airy and convenient; but if the stomach is fed with sour bread and burnt coffee, it will raise such rebellions that the eyes will see no beauty anywhere. Now in the little tour that you and I have been taking this summer, I have been thinking of the great abundance of splendid material we have in America, compared with the poor cooking. How often, in our stoppings, we have sat down to tables loaded with material, originally of the very best kind, which had been so spoiled in the treatment that there was really nothing to eat! Green biscuits with acrid spots of alkali, — sour yeast-bread, — meat slowly simmered in fat till it seemed like grease itself, and slowly congealing in cold grease, — and above all, that unpardonable enormity, strong butter! How often I have longed to show people what might have been done with the raw material out of which all these monstrosities were concocted!"

"My dear," said I, "you are driving me upon delicate ground. Would you have your husband appear in public with that most opprobrious badge of the domestic furies, a dishcloth pinned to his coat-tail? It is coming to exactly the point I have always predicted, Mrs. Crowfield : you must write yourself. I always told you that you could write far better than I, if you would only try. Only sit down and write as you sometimes talk to me, and I might hang up my pen by the side of 'Uncle Ned's' fiddle and bow."

"O, nonsense!" said my wife. "I never could write. I know what ought to be said, and I could *say* it to any one ; but my ideas freeze in the pen, cramp in my fingers, and make my brain seem like heavy bread. I was born for extemporary speaking. Besides, I think the best things on all subjects in this world of ours are said, not by the practical workers, but by the careful observers."

"Mrs. Crowfield, that remark is as good as if I had made it myself," said I. "It is true that I have been all my life a speculator and observer in all domestic matters, having them so confidentially under my eye in our own household ; and so, if I write on a pure woman's matter, it must be understood that I am only your pen and mouth-piece, — only giving tangible form to wisdom which I have derived from you."

So down I sat and scribbled, while my sovereign lady quietly stitched by my side. And here I tell my

reader that I write on such a subject under protest, —
declaring again my conviction, that, if my wife only
believed in herself as firmly as I do, she would write
so that nobody would ever want to listen to me again.

COOKERY.

WE in America have the raw material of provision
in greater abundance than any other nation.   There
is no country where an ample, well-furnished table is
more easily spread, and for that reason, perhaps, none
where the bounties of Providence are more generally
neglected.   I do not mean to say that the traveller
through the length and breadth of our land could not,
on the whole, find an average of comfortable subsist-
ence ; yet, considering that our resources are greater
than those of any other civilized people, our results
are comparatively poorer.

It is said, that, a list of the summer vegetables which
are exhibited on New York hotel-tables being shown
to a French *artiste*, he declared that to serve such a
dinner properly would take till midnight.   I recollect
how I was once struck with our national plenteous-
ness, on returning from a Continental tour, and going
directly from the ship to a New York hotel, in the
bounteous season of autumn.   For months I had been
habituated to my neat little bits of chop or poultry
garnished with the inevitable cauliflower or potato,

which seemed to be the sole possibility after the reign of green-peas was over ; now I sat down all at once to a carnival of vegetables : ripe, juicy tomatoes, raw or cooked ; cucumbers in brittle slices ; rich, yellow sweet-potatoes ; broad Lima-beans, and beans of other and various names ; tempting ears of Indian-corn steaming in enormous piles, and great smoking tureens of the savory succotash, an Indian gift to the table for which civilization need not blush ; sliced egg-plant in delicate fritters ; and marrow-squashes, of creamy pulp and sweetness : a rich variety, embarrassing to the appetite, and perplexing to the choice. Verily, the thought has often impressed itself on my mind that the vegetarian doctrine preached in America left a man quite as much as he had capacity to eat or enjoy, and that in the midst of such tantalizing abundance he really lost the apology which elsewhere bears him out in preying upon his less gifted and accomplished animal neighbors.

But with all this, the American table, taken as a whole, is inferior to that of England or France. It presents a fine abundance of material, carelessly and poorly treated. The management of food is nowhere in the world, perhaps, more slovenly and wasteful. Everything betokens that want of care that waits on abundance ; there are great capabilities and poor execution. A tourist through England can seldom fail,

at the quietest country-inn, of finding himself served
with the essentials of English table-comfort, — his
mutton-chop done to a turn, his steaming little private
apparatus for concocting his own tea, his choice pot
of marmalade or slice of cold ham, and his delicate
rolls and creamy butter, all served with care and neatness. In France, one never asks in vain for delicious
café-au-lait, good bread and butter, a nice omelet, or
some savory little portion of meat with a French name.
But to a tourist taking like chance in American coun-
try-fare, what is the prospect? What is the coffee?
what the tea? and the meat? and above all, the butter?

In lecturing on cookery, as on house-building, I
divide the subject into not four, but five grand elements : first, Bread ; second, Butter ; third, Meat ;
fourth, Vegetables ; and fifth, Tea, — by which I mean,
generically, all sorts of warm, comfortable drinks served
out in teacups, whether they be called tea, coffee,
chocolate, broma, or what not.

I affirm, that, if these five departments are all perfect, the great ends of domestic cookery are answered,
so far as the comfort and well-being of life are concerned. I am aware that there exists another department, which is often regarded by culinary amateurs
and young aspirants as the higher branch and very
collegiate course of practical cookery ; to wit, Confec-
tionery, by which I mean to designate all pleasing

and complicated compounds of sweets and spices, devised not for health and nourishment, and strongly suspected of interfering with both, — mere tolerated gratifications of the palate, which we eat, not with the expectation of being benefited, but only with the hope of not being injured by them. In this large department rank all sort of cakes, pies, preserves, ices, etc. I shall have a word or two to say under this head before I have done. I only remark now, that in my tours about the country I have often had a virulent ill-will excited towards these works of culinary supererogation, because I thought their excellence was attained by treading under foot and disregarding the five grand essentials. I have sat at many a table garnished with three or four kinds of well-made cake, compounded with citron and spices and all imaginable good things, where the meat was tough and greasy, the bread some hot preparation of flour, lard, saleratus, and acid, and the butter unutterably detestable. At such tables I have thought, that, if the mistress of the feast had given the care, time, and labor to preparing the simple items of bread, butter, and meat, that she evidently had given to the preparation of these extras, the lot of a traveller might be much more comfortable. Evidently, she never had thought of these common articles as constituting a good table. So. long as she had puff pastry, rich black cake, clear jelly, and preserves, she seemed to consider that such unimportant matters as bread, butter, and meat could take care of themselves. It is·the same inattention to common things as that which leads people to build houses with stone fronts and window-caps and expensive front-door trimmings, without bathing-rooms or fireplaces or ventilators.

Those·who go into the country looking for summer board in farm-houses know perfectly well that a table where the butter is always fresh, the tea and coffee of the best kinds and well made, and the meats properly kept, dressed, and served, is the one table of a hundred, the fabulous enchanted island. It seems impossible to get the idea into the minds of people that what is called common food, carefully prepared, becomes, in virtue of that very care and attention, a delicacy, superseding the necessity of artificially compounded dainties.

To begin, then, with the very foundation of a good table, — *Bread :* What ought it to be ? It should be light, sweet, and tender.

This matter of lightness is the distinctive line between savage and civilized bread. The savage mixes simple flour and water into balls of paste, which he throws into boiling water, and which come out solid, glutinous masses, of which his common saying is, " Man eat dis, he no die," — which a facetious traveller who was obliged to subsist on it interpreted to mean, "Dis no kill you, nothing will." In short, it requires the stomach of a wild animal or of a savage to digest this primitive form of bread, and of course more or less attention in all civilized modes of bread-making is given to producing lightness. By lightness is meant simply that the particles are to be separated from each other by little holes or air-cells; and all the different methods of making light bread are neither more nor less than the formation in bread of these air-cells.

So far as we know, there are four practicable methods of aerating bread; namely, by fermentation, — by effervescence of an acid and an alkali, — by aerated egg, or egg which has been filled with air by the process of beating, — and lastly, by pressure of some gaseous substance into the paste, by a process much resembling the impregnation of water in a soda-fountain. All these have one and the same object, — to give us the cooked particles of our flour separated by such permanent air-cells as will enable the stomach more readily to digest them.

A very common mode of aerating bread, in America, is by the effervescence of an acid and an alkali in the flour. The carbonic acid gas thus formed produces minute air-cells in the bread, or, as the cook says, makes it light. When this process is performed with exact attention to chemical laws, so that the acid and alkali completely neutralize each other, leaving no overplus of either, the result is often very palatable. The difficulty is, that this is a happy conjunction of circumstances which seldom occurs. The acid most commonly employed is that of sour milk, and, as milk has many degrees of sourness, the rule of a certain quantity of alkali to the pint must necessarily produce very different results at different times. As an actual fact, where this mode of making bread prevails, as we lament to say it does to a great extent in this country, one finds five cases of failure to one of success. It is a woful thing that the daughters of New England have abandoned the old respectable mode of yeast-brewing and bread-raising for this specious substitute, so easily made, and so seldom well made. The green, clammy, acrid substance, called biscuit, which many of our worthy republicans are obliged to eat in these days, is wholly unworthy of the men and women of the Republic. Good patriots ought not to be put off in that way, — they deserve better fare.

As an occasional variety, as a household convenience for obtaining bread or biscuit at a moment's notice, the process of effervescence may be retained ; but we earnestly entreat American housekeepers, in Scriptural language, to stand in the way and ask for the old paths, and return to the good yeast-bread of their sainted grandmothers.

If acid and alkali must be used, by all means let them be mixed in due proportions. No cook should be left to guess and judge for herself about this matter. There is an article, called "Preston's Infallible Yeast-Powder," which is made by chemical rule, and produces very perfect results. The use of this obviates the worst dangers in making bread by effervescence.

Of all processes of aeration in bread-making, the oldest and most time-honored is by fermentation. That this was known in the days of our Saviour is evident from the forcible simile in which he compares the silent permeating force of truth in human society to the very familiar household process of raising bread by a little yeast.

There is, however, one species of yeast, much used in some parts of the country, against which I have to enter my protest. It is called salt-risings, or milk-risings, and is made by mixing flour, milk, and a little salt together, and leaving them to ferment. The bread thus produced is often very attractive, when new and made with great care. It is white and delicate, with fine, even air-cells. It has, however, when kept, some characteristics which remind us of the terms in which our old English Bible describes the effect of keeping the manna of the ancient Israelites, which we are informed, in words more explicit than agreeable, " stank, and bred worms." If salt-rising bread does not fulfil the whole of this unpleasant description, it certainly does emphatically a part of it. The smell which it has in baking, and when more than a day old, suggests.the inquiry, whether it is the saccharine or the putrid fermentation with which it is raised. Whoever breaks a piece of it after a day or two will often see minute filaments or clammy strings drawing out from the fragments, which, with the unmistakable smell, will cause him to pause before consummating a nearer acquaintance.

The fermentation of flour by means of brewer's or distiller's yeast produces, if rightly managed, results far more palatable and wholesome. The only requisites for success in it are, first, good materials, and, second, great care in a few small things. There are certain low-priced or damaged kinds of flour which can never by any kind of domestic chemistry be made into good bread ; and to those persons whose stomachs forbid them to eat gummy, glutinous paste, under the name of bread, there is no economy in buying these poor brands, even at half the price of good flour.

But good flour and good yeast being supposed, with a temperature favorable to the development of fermentation, the whole success of the process depends on the thorough diffusion of the proper proportion of yeast through the whole mass, and on stopping the subsequent fermentation at the precise and fortunate point. The true housewife makes her bread the sovereign of her kitchen, — its behests must be attended to in all critical points and moments, no matter what else be postponed. She who attends to her bread when she has done this, and arranged that, and performed the other, very often finds that the forces of nature will not wait for her. The snowy mass, perfectly mixed, kneaded with câre and strength, rises in its beautiful perfection till the moment comes for fixing the air-cells by baking. A few minutes now, and the acetous fermentation will begin, and the whole result be spoiled. Many bread-makers pass in utter carelessness over this sacred and mysterious boundary. Their oven has cake in it, or they are skimming jelly, or attending to some other of the so-called higher branches of cookery, while the bread is quickly passing into the acetous stage. At last, when they are ready to attend to it, they find that it has been going its own way, — it is so sour that the pungent smell is plainly perceptible. Now the saleratus-bottle is handed down, and a quantity of the dissolved alkali mixed with the paste, — an expedient sometimes making itself too manifest by greenish streaks or small acrid spots in the bread. As the result, we have a beautiful article spoiled, — bread without sweetness, if not absolutely sour.

In the view of many, lightness is the only property required in this article. The delicate, refined sweetness which exists in carefully kneaded bread, baked just before it passes to the extreme point of fermentation, is something of which they have no conception; and thus they will even regard this process of spoiling the paste by the acetous fermentation, and then rectifying that acid by effervescence with an alkali, as something positively meritorious. How else can they value and relish bakers' loaves, such as some are, drugged with ammonia and other disagreeable things, light indeed, so light that they seem to have neither weight nor substance, but with no more sweetness or taste than so much white cotton?

Some persons prepare bread for the oven by simply mixing it in the mass, without kneading, pouring it into pans, and suffering it to rise there. The air-cells in bread thus prepared are coarse and uneven; the bread is as inferior in delicacy and nicety to that which is well kneaded as a raw Irish servant to a perfectly educated and refined lady. The process of kneading seems to impart an evenness to the minute air-cells, a fineness of texture, and a tenderness and pliability to the whole substance, that can be gained in no other way.

The divine principle of beauty has its reign over bread as well as over all other things; it has its laws of æsthetics; and that bread which is so prepared that it can be formed into separate and well-proportioned loaves, each one carefully worked and moulded, will develop the most beautiful results. After being moulded, the loaves should stand a little while, just long enough to allow the fermentation going on in them to expand each little air-cell to the point at which it stood before it was worked down, and then they should be immediately put into the oven.

Many a good thing, however, is spoiled in the oven. We cannot but regret, for the sake of bread, that our old steady brick ovens have been almost universally superseded by those of ranges and cooking-stoves, which are infinite in their caprices, and forbid all general rules. One thing, however, may be borne in mind as a principle, — that the excellence of bread in all its varieties, plain or sweetened, depends on the perfection of its air-cells, whether produced by yeast, egg, or effervescence; that one of the objects of baking is to fix these air-cells, and that the quicker this can be done through the whole mass, the better will the result be. When cake or bread is made heavy by baking too quickly, it is because the immediate formation of the top crust hinders the exhaling of the moisture in the centre, and prevents the air-cells from cooking. The weight also of the crust pressing down on the doughy air-cells below destroys them, producing that horror of good cooks, a heavy streak. The problem in baking, then, is the quick application of heat rather below than above the loaf, and its steady continuance till all the air-cells are thoroughly dried into permanent consistency. Every housewife must watch her own oven to know how this can be best accomplished.

Bread-making can be cultivated to any extent as a fine art, — and the various kinds of biscuit, tea-rusks, twists, rolls, into which bread may be made, are much better worth a housekeeper's ambition than the getting-up of rich and expensive cake or confections. There are also varieties of material which are rich in good effects. Unbolted flour, altogether more wholesome than the fine wheat, and when properly prepared more palatable, — rye-flour and corn-meal, each affording a thousand attractive possibilities, — each and all of these come under the general laws of bread-stuffs, and are worth a careful attention.

A peculiarity of our American table, particularly in the Southern and Western States, is the constant exhibition of various preparations of hot bread. In many families of the South and West, bread in loaves to be eaten cold is an article quite unknown. The effect of this kind of diet upon the health has formed a frequent subject of remark among travellers ; but only those know the full mischiefs of it who have been compelled to sojourn for a length of time in families where it is maintained. The unknown horrors of dyspepsia from bad bread are a topic over which we willingly draw a veil.

Next to Bread comes *Butter*, — on which we have to say, that, when we remember what butter is in civilized Europe, and compare it with what it is in America, we wonder at the forbearance and lenity of travellers in their strictures on our national commissariat.

Butter, in England, France, and Italy, is simply solidified cream, with all the sweetness of the cream in its taste, freshly churned each day, and unadulterated by salt. At the present moment, when salt is five cents a pound and butter fifty, we Americans are paying, I should judge from the taste, for about one pound of salt to every ten of butter, and those of us who have eaten the butter of France and England do this with rueful recollections.

There is, it is true, an article of butter made in the American style with salt, which, in its own kind and way, has a merit not inferior to that of England and France. Many prefer it, and it certainly takes a rank equally respectable with the other. It is yellow, hard, and worked so perfectly free from every particle of buttermilk that it might make the voyage of the world without spoiling. It is salted, but salted with care and delicacy, so that it may be a question whether even a fastidious Englishman might not prefer its golden solidity to the white, creamy freshness of his own. Now. I am not for universal imitation of foreign customs, and where I find this butter made perfectly, I call it our American style, and am not ashamed of it. I only regret that this article is the exception, and not the rule, on our tables. When I reflect on the possibilities which beset the delicate stomach in this line, I do not wonder that my venerated friend Dr. Mussey used to close his counsels to invalids with the direction, "And don't eat grease on your bread."

America must, I think, have the credit of manufacturing and putting into market more bad butter than all that is made in all the rest of the world together. The varieties of bad tastes and smells which prevail in it are quite a study. This has a cheesy taste, that a mouldy, — this is flavored with cabbage, and that again with turnip, and another has the strong, sharp savor of rancid animal fat. These varieties, I presume, come from the practice of churning only at long intervals, and keeping the cream meanwhile in unventilated cellars or dairies, the air of which is loaded with the effluvia of vegetable substances. No domestic articles are so sympathetic as those of the milk tribe : they readily take on the smell and taste of any neighboring substance, and hence the infinite variety of flavors on which one mournfully muses who has late in autumn to taste twenty firkins of butter in hopes of finding one which will simply not be intolerable on his winter table.

A matter for despair as regards bad butter is that at the tables where it is used it stands sentinel at the door to bar your way to every other kind of food. You turn from your dreadful half-slice of bread, which fills your mouth with bitterness, to your beef-steak, which proves virulent with the same poison ; you think to take refuge in vegetable diet, and find the butter in the string-beans, and polluting the innocence of early peas, — it is in the corn, in the succotash, in the squash, — the beets swim in it, the onions have it poured over them. Hungry and miserable, you think to solace yourself at the dessert, — but the pastry is cursed, the cake is acrid with the same plague. You are ready to howl with despair, and your misery is great upon you, — especially if this is a table where you have taken board for three months with your delicate wife and four small children. Your case is dreadful, — and it is hopeless, because long usage and habit have rendered your host perfectly incapable of discovering what is the matter. " Don't like the butter, Sir? I assure you I paid an extra price for it, and it 's the very best in the market. I looked over as many as a hundred tubs, and picked out this one." You are dumb, but not less despairing.

Yet the process of making good butter is a very simple one. To keep the cream in a perfectly pure, cool atmosphere, to churn while it is yet sweet, to work out the buttermilk thoroughly, and to add salt with such discretion as not to ruin the fine, delicate flavor of the fresh cream, — all this is quite simple, so simple that one wonders at thousands and millions of pounds of butter yearly manufactured which are merely a hobgoblin-bewitchment of cream into foul and loathsome poisons.

The third head of my discourse is that of *Meat*, of which America furnishes, in the gross material, enough to spread our tables royally, were it well cared for and served.

The faults in the meat generally furnished to us are, first, that it is too new. A beefsteak, which three or four days of keeping might render practicable, is served up to us palpitating with freshness, with all the toughness of animal muscle yet warm. In the Western country, the traveller, on approaching an hotel, is often saluted by the last shrieks of the chickens which half an hour afterward are presented to him *à la* spread-eagle for his dinner. The example of the Father of the Faithful, most wholesome to be followed in so many respects, is imitated only in the celerity with which the young calf, tender and good, was transformed into an edible dish for hospitable purposes. But what might be good housekeeping in a nomadic Emir, in days when refrigerators were yet in the future, ought not to be so closely imitated as it often is in our own land.

In the next place, there is a woful lack of nicety in the butcher's work of cutting and preparing meat. Who that remembers the neatly trimmed mutton-chop of an English inn, or the artistic little circle of lamb-chop fried in bread-crumbs coiled around a tempting centre of spinach which can always be found in France, can recognize any family-resemblance to these dapper civilized preparations in those coarse, roughly hacked strips of bone, gristle, and meat which are commonly called mutton-chop in America? There seems to be a large dish of something resembling meat, in which each fragment has about two or three edible morsels, the rest being composed of dry and burnt skin, fat, and ragged bone.

Is it not time that civilization should learn to demand somewhat more care and nicety in the modes of preparing what is to be cooked and eaten? Might not some of the refinement and trimness which characterize the preparations of the European market be with advantage introduced into our own? The housekeeper who wishes to garnish her table with some of those nice things is stopped in the outset by the butcher. Except in our large cities, where some foreign travel may have created the demand, it seems impossible to get much in this line that is properly prepared.

I am aware, that, if this is urged on the score of æsthetics, the ready reply will be, " O, we can't give time here in America to go into niceties and French whim-whams!" But the French mode of doing almost all practical things is based on that true philosophy and utilitarian good sense which characterize that seemingly thoughtless people. Nowhere is economy a more careful study, and their market is artistically arranged to this end. The rule is so to cut their meats that no portion designed to be cooked in a certain manner shall have wasteful appendages which that mode of cooking will spoil. The French soup-kettle stands ever ready to receive the bones, the thin fibrous flaps, the sinewy and gristly portions, which are so often included in our roasts or broilings, which fill our plates with unsightly *débris*, and finally make an amount of blank waste for which we pay our butcher the same price that we pay for what we have eaten.

The dead waste of our clumsy, coarse way of cutting meats is immense. For example, at the beginning of the present season, the part of a lamb denominated leg and loin, or hind-quarter, sold for thirty cents a pound. Now this includes, besides the thick, fleshy portions, a quantity of bone, sinew, and thin fibrous substance, constituting full one third of the whole weight. If we put it into the oven entire, in the usual manner, we have the thin parts overdone, and the skinny and fibrous parts utterly dried up, by the application of the amount of heat necessary to cook the thick portion. Supposing the joint to weigh six pounds, at thirty cents, and that one third of the weight is so treated as to become perfectly useless, we throw away sixty cents. Of a piece of beef at twenty-five cents a pound, fifty cents' worth is often lost in bone, fat, and burnt skin.

The fact is, this way of selling and cooking meat in large, gross portions is of English origin, and belongs to a country where all the customs of society spring from a class who have no particular occasion for economy. The practice of minute and delicate division comes from a nation which acknowledges the need of economy, and has made it a study. A quarter of lamb in this mode of division would be sold in three nicely prepared portions. The thick part would be sold by itself, for a neat, compact little roast ; the rib-bones would be artistically separated, and all the edible matters scraped away would form those delicate dishes of lamb-chop, which, fried in bread-crumbs to a golden brown, are so ornamental and so palatable a side-dish ; the trimmings which remain after this division would be destined to the soup-kettle or stew-pan. In a French market is a little portion for every purse, and the far-famed and delicately flavored soups and stews which have arisen out of French economy are a study worth a housekeeper's attention. Not one atom of food is wasted in the French modes of preparation ; even tough animal cartilages and sinews, instead of appearing burned and blackened in company with the roast meat to which they happen to be related, are treated according to their own laws, and come out either in savory soups, or those fine, clear meat-jellies which form a garnish no less agreeable to the eye than palatable to the taste.

Whether this careful, economical, practical style of meat-cooking can ever to any great extent be introduced into our kitchens now is a question. Our butchers are against it ; our servants are wedded to the old wholesale wasteful ways, which seem to them easier because they are accustomed to them. A cook who will keep and properly tend a soup-kettle which shall receive and utilize all that the coarse preparations of the butcher would require her to trim away, who understands the art of making the most of all these remains, is a treasure scarcely to be hoped for. If such things are to be done, it must be primarily through the educated brain of cultivated women who do not scorn to turn their culture and refinement upon domestic problems.

When meats have been properly divided, so that each portion can receive its own appropriate style of treatment, next comes the consideration of the modes of cooking. These may be divided into two great general classes : those where it is desired to keep the juices within the meat, as in baking, broiling, and frying, — and those whose object is to extract the juice and dissolve the fibre, as in the making of soups and stews. In the first class of operations, the process must be as rapid as may consist with the thorough cooking of all the particles. In this branch of cookery, doing quickly is doing well. The fire must be brisk, the attention alert. The introduction of cooking-stoves offers to careless domestics facilities for gradually drying-up meats, and despoiling them of all flavor and nutriment, — facilities which appear to be very generally laid hold of. They have almost banished the genuine, old-fashioned roast-meat from our tables, and left in its stead dried meats with their most precious and nutritive juices evaporated. How few cooks, unassisted, are competent to the simple process of broiling a beefsteak or mutton-chop ! how very generally one has to choose between these meats gradually dried away, or burned on the outside and raw within ! Yet in England these articles *never* come on table done amiss ; their perfect cooking is as absolute a certainty as the rising of the sun.

No one of these rapid processes of cooking, however, is so generally abused as frying. The frying-pan has awful sins to answer for. What untold horrors of dyspepsia have arisen from its smoky depths, like the ghosts from witches' caldrons ! The fizzle of frying meat is as a warning knell on many an ear, saying, " Touch not, taste not, if you would not burn and writhe ! "

Yet those who have travelled abroad remember that some of the lightest, most palatable, and most digestible preparations of meat have come from this dangerous source. But we fancy quite other rites and ceremonies inaugurated the process, and quite other hands performed its offices, than those known to our kitchens. Probably the delicate *côtelettes* of France are not flopped down into half-melted grease, there gradually to warm and soak and fizzle, while Biddy goes in and out on her other ministrations, till finally, when thoroughly saturated, and dinner-hour impends, she bethinks herself, and crowds the fire below to a roaring heat, and finishes the process by a smart burn, involving the kitchen and surrounding precincts in volumes of Stygian gloom.

From such preparations has arisen the very current medical opinion that fried meats are indigestible. They are indigestible, if they are greasy ; but French cooks have taught us that a thing has no more need to be greasy because emerging from grease than Venus had to be salt because she rose from the sea.

There are two ways of frying employed by the French cook. One is, to immerse the article to be cooked in *boiling* fat, with an emphasis on the present participle, — and the philosophical principle is, so immediately to crisp every pore, at the first moment or two of immersion, as effectually to seal the interior against the intrusion of greasy particles ; it can then remain as long as may be necessary thoroughly to cook it, without imbibing any more of the boiling fluid than if it were inclosed in an egg-shell. The other method is to rub a perfectly smooth iron surface with just enough of some oily substance to prevent the meat from adhering, and cook it with a quick heat, as cakes are baked on a griddle. In both these cases there must be the most rapid application of heat that can be made without burning, and by the adroitness shown in working out this problem the skill of the cook is tested. Any one whose cook attains this important secret will find fried things quite as digestible and often more palatable than any other.

In the second department of meat-cookery, to wit, the slow and gradual application of heat for the softening and dissolution of its fibre and the extraction of its juices, common cooks are equally untrained. Where is the so-called cook who understands how to prepare soups and stews? These are precisely the articles in which a French kitchen excels. The soup-kettle, made with a double bottom, to prevent burning, is a permanent, ever-present institution, and the coarsest and most impracticable meats distilled through that alembic come out again in soups, jellies, or savory stews. The toughest cartilage, even the bones, being first cracked, are here made to give forth their hidden virtues, and to rise in delicate and appetizing forms. One great law governs all these preparations : the application of heat must be gradual, steady, long protracted, never reaching the point of active boiling. Hours of quiet simmering dissolve all dissoluble parts, soften the sternest fibre, and unlock every minute cell in which Nature has stored away her treasures of nourishment. This careful and protracted application of heat and the skilful use of flavors constitute the two main points in all those nice preparations of meat for which the French have so many names, — processes by which a delicacy can be imparted to the coarsest and cheapest food superior to that of the finest articles under less philosophic treatment.

French soups and stews are a study, — and they would not be an unprofitable one to any person who wishes to live with comfort and even elegance on small means.

John Bull looks down from the sublime of ten thousand a year on French kickshaws, as he calls them : — "Give me my meat cooked so I may know what it is !" An ox roasted whole is dear to John's soul, and his kitchen-arrangements are Titanic. What magnificent rounds and sirloins of beef, revolving on self-regulating spits, with a rich click of satisfaction, before grates piled with roaring fires ! Let us do justice to the royal cheer. Nowhere are the charms of pure, unadulterated animal food set forth in more imposing style. For John is rich, and what does he care for odds and ends and parings? Has he not all the beasts of the forest, and the cattle on a thousand hills? What does he want of economy ? But his brother Jean has not ten thousand pounds a year, — nothing like it ; but he makes up for the slenderness of his purse by boundless fertility of invention and delicacy of practice. John began sneering at Jean's soups and ragouts, but all John's modern sons and daughters send to Jean for their cooks, and the sirloins of England rise up and do obeisance to this Joseph with a white apron who comes to rule in their kitchens.

There is no animal fibre that will not yield itself up to long-continued, steady heat. But the difficulty with almost any of the common servants who call themselves cooks is, that they have not the smallest notion of the philosophy of the application of heat. Such a one will complacently tell you concerning certain meats, that the harder you boil them the harder they grow, — an obvious fact, which, under her mode of treatment, by an indiscriminate galloping boil, has frequently come under her personal observation. If you tell her that such meat must stand for six hours in a heat just below the boiling-point, she will probably answer, "Yes, Ma'am," and go on her own way. Or she will let it stand till it burns to the bottom of the kettle, — a most common termination of the experiment. The only way to make sure of the matter is either to import a French kettle, or to fit into an ordinary kettle a false bottom, such as any tinman may make, that shall leave a space of an inch or two between the meat and the fire. This kettle may be maintained as a constant *habitué* of the range, and into it the cook may be instructed to throw all the fibrous trimmings of meat, all the gristle, tendons, and bones, having previously broken up these last with a mallet.

Such a kettle will furnish the basis for clear, rich soups or other palatable dishes. Clear soup consists of the dissolved juices of the meat and gelatine of the bones, cleared from the fat and fibrous portions by straining when cold. The grease, which rises to the top of the fluid, may thus be easily removed. In a stew, on the contrary, you boil down this soup till it permeates the fibre which long exposure to heat has softened. All that remains, after the proper preparation of the fibre and juices, is the flavoring, and it is in this, particularly, that French soups excel those of America and England and all the world.

English and American soups are often heavy and hot with spices. There are appreciable tastes in them. They burn your mouth with cayenne or clove or allspice. You can tell at once what is in them, oftentimes to your sorrow. But a French soup has a flavor which one recognizes at once as delicious, yet not to be characterized as due to any single condiment; it is the just blending of many things. The same remark applies to all their stews, ragouts, and other delicate preparations. No cook will ever study these flavors; but perhaps many cooks' mistresses may, and thus be able to impart delicacy and comfort to economy.

As to those things called hashes, commonly manufactured by unwatched, untaught cooks, out of the remains of yesterday's repast, let us not dwell too closely on their memory, — compounds of meat, gristle, skin, fat, and burnt fibre, with a handful of pepper and salt flung at them, dredged with lumpy flour, watered from the spout of the tea-kettle, and left to simmer at the cook's convenience while she is otherwise occupied. Such are the best performances a housekeeper can hope for from an untrained cook.

But the cunningly devised minces, the artful preparations choicely flavored, which may be made of yesterday's repast, — by these is the true domestic artist known. No cook untaught by an educated brain ever makes these, and yet economy is a great gainer by them.

As regards the department of *Vegetables*, their number and variety in America are so great that a table might almost be furnished by these alone. Generally speaking, their cooking is a more simple art, and therefore more likely to be found satisfactorily performed, than that of meats. If only they are not drenched with rancid butter, their own native excellence makes itself known in most of the ordinary modes of preparation.

There is, however, one exception.

Our stanch old friend, the potato, is to other vegetables what bread is on the table. Like bread, it is held as a sort of *sine-qua-non;* like that, it may be made invariably palatable by a little care in a few plain particulars, through neglect of which it often becomes intolerable. The soggy, waxy, indigestible viand that often appears in the potato-dish is a downright sacrifice of the better nature of this vegetable.

The potato, nutritive and harmless as it appears, belongs to a family suspected of very dangerous traits. It is a family-connection of the deadly-nightshade and other ill-reputed gentry, and sometimes shows strange proclivities to evil, — now breaking out uproariously, as in the noted potato-rot, and now more covertly, in various evil affections. For this reason scientific directors bid us beware of the water in which potatoes are boiled, — into which, it appears, the evil principle is drawn off; and they caution us not to shred them into stews without previously suffering the slices to lie for an hour or so in salt and water. These cautions are worth attention.

The most usual modes of preparing the potato for the table are by roasting or boiling. These processes are so simple that it is commonly supposed every

Q

cook understands them without special directions ;
and yet there is scarcely an uninstructed cook who
can boil or roast a potato.

A good roasted potato is a delicacy worth a dozen
compositions of the cook-book ; yet when we ask for
it, what burnt, shrivelled abortions are presented to
us ! Biddy rushes to her potato-basket and pours
out two dozen of different sizes, some having in them
three times the amount of matter of others. These
being washed, she tumbles them into her oven at a
leisure interval, and there lets them lie till it is time
to serve breakfast, whenever that may be. As a
result, if the largest are cooked, the smallest are
presented in cinders, and the intermediate sizes are
withered and watery. Nothing is so utterly ruined
by a few moments of overdoing. That which at the
right moment was plump with mealy richness, a quarter of an hour later shrivels and becomes watery, —
and it is in this state that roast potatoes are most
frequently served.

In the same manner we have seen boiled potatoes
from an untaught cook coming upon the table like
lumps of yellow wax, — and the same article, the day
after, under the directions of a skilful mistress, appearing in snowy balls of powdery lightness. In the
one case, they were thrown in their skins into water,
and suffered to soak or boil, as the case might be, at

the cook's leisure, and after they were boiled to stand in the water till she was ready to peel them. In the other case, the potatoes being first peeled were boiled as quickly as possible in salted water, which the moment they were done was drained off, and then they were gently shaken for a minute or two over the fire to dry them still more thoroughly. We have never yet seen the potato so depraved and given over to evil that could not be reclaimed by this mode of treatment.

As to fried potatoes, who that remembers the crisp, golden slices of the French restaurant, thin as wafers and light as snow-flakes, does not speak respectfully of them? What cousinship with these have those coarse, greasy masses of sliced potato, wholly soggy and partly burnt, to which we are treated under the name of fried potatoes *à la* America? In our cities the restaurants are introducing the French article to great acceptance, and to the vindication of the fair fame of this queen of vegetables.

Finally, I arrive at the last great head of my subject, to wit, TEA, — meaning thereby, as before observed, what our Hibernian friend did in the inquiry, "Will y'r Honor take 'tay tay' or coffee tay?"

I am not about to enter into the merits of the

great tea-and-coffee controversy, or say whether these
substances are or áre not wholesome. I treat of
them as actual existences, and speak only of the
modes of making the most of them.

The French coffee is reputed the best in the world;
and a thousand voices have asked, What is it about
the French coffee?

In the first place, then, the French coffee is coffee,
and not chiccory, or rye, or beans, or peas. In the
second place, it is freshly roasted, whenever made, —
roasted with great care and evenness in a little revolving cylinder which makes part of the furniture of every
kitchen, and which keeps in the aroma of the berry.
It is never overdone, so as to destroy the coffee-flavor,
which is in nine cases out of ten the fault of the coffee
we meet with. Then it is ground, and placed in a
coffee-pot with a filter, through which it percolates in
clear drops, the coffee-pot standing on a heated stove to
maintain the temperature. The nose of the coffee-pot
is stopped up to prevent the escape of the aroma during
this process. The extract thus obtained is a perfectly
clear, dark fluid, known as *café noir*, or black coffee.
It is black only because of its strength, being in fact
almost the very essential oil of coffee. A table-spoon-
ful of this in boiled milk would make what is ordi-
narily called a strong cup of coffee. The boiled milk
is prepared with no less care. It must be fresh and

·new, not merely warmed or even brought to the boiling-point, but slowly simmered till it attains a thick,
creamy richness.   The coffee mixed with this, and
sweetened with that sparkling beet-root sugar which
ornaments a French table, is the celebrated *café-au-
lait*, the name of which has gone round the world.

As we look to France for the best coffee, so we
must look to England for the perfection of tea.   The
tea-kettle is as much an English institution as aristocracy or the Prayer-Book; and when one wants to
know exactly how tea should be made, one has only
to ask how a fine old English housekeeper makes it.

The first article of her faith is that the water must
not merely be hot, not merely *have boiled* a few moments since, but be actually *boiling* at the moment it
touches the tea.   Hence, though servants in England are vastly better trained than with us, this delicate mystery is seldom left to their hands.   Tea-mak-
ing belongs to the drawing-room, and high-born ladies
·preside at "the bubbling and loud-hissing urn," and
see that all due rites and solemnities are properly
performed, — that the cups are hot, and that the in-
fused tea waits the exact time before the libations
commence.   O, ye dear old English tea-tables, resorts
of the kindest-hearted hospitality in the world ! we
still cherish your memory, even though you do not
say pleasant things of us there.   One of these days

you will think better of us. Of late, the introduction
of English breakfast-tea has raised a new sect among
the tea-drinkers, reversing some of the old canons.
Breakfast-tea must be boiled! Unlike the delicate
article of olden time, which required only a momen-
tary infusion to develop its richness, this requires a
longer and severer treatment to bring out its strength,
— thus confusing all the established usages, and
throwing the work into the hands of the cook in the
kitchen.

The faults of tea, as too commonly found at our
hotels and boarding-houses, are that it is made in
every way the reverse of what it should be. The
water is hot, perhaps, but not boiling; the tea has
a general flat, stale, smoky taste, devoid of life or
spirit; and it is served, usually, with thin milk, instead
of cream. Cream is as essential to the richness of
tea as of coffee. We could wish that the English
fashion might generally prevail, of giving the traveller
his own kettle of boiling water and his own tea-chest,
and letting him make tea for himself. At all events,
he would then be sure of one merit in his tea, — it
would be hot, a very simple and obvious virtue, but
one very seldom obtained.

Chocolate is a French and Spanish article, and one
seldom served on American tables. We, in America,
however, make an article every way equal to any

which can be imported from Paris, and he who buys
Baker's best vanilla-chocolate may rest assured that
no foreign land can furnish anything better. A very
rich and delicious beverage may be made by dissolv-
ing this in milk slowly boiled down after the French
fashion.

I have now gone over all the ground I laid out,
as comprising the great first principles of cookery;
and I would here modestly offer the opinion that a
table where all these principles are carefully observed
would need few dainties. The struggle after so-called
delicacies comes from the poorness of common things.
Perfect bread and butter would soon drive cake out
of the field; it has done so in many families. Nevertheless, I have a word to say under the head of *Con-
fectionery*, meaning by this the whole range of ornamental cookery, — or pastry, ices, jellies, preserves,
etc. The art of making all these very perfectly is far
better understood in America than the art of common
cooking.

There are more women who know how to make
good cake than good bread, — more who can furnish
you with a good ice-cream than a well-cooked mutton-
chop; a fair charlotte-russe is easier to come by than
a perfect cup of coffee, and you shall find a sparkling
jelly to your dessert where you sighed in vain for so
simple a luxury as a well-cooked potato.

Our fair countrywomen might rest upon their laurels
in these higher fields, and turn their great energy and
ingenuity to the study of essentials. To do common
things perfectly is far better worth our endeavor than
to do uncommon things respectably. We Americans
in many things as yet have been a little inclined to
begin making our shirt at the ruffle; but, nevertheless, when we set about it, we can make the shirt
as nicely as anybody, — it needs only that we turn
our attention to it, resolved, that, ruffle or no ruffle,
the shirt we will have.

I have also a few words to say as to the prevalent
ideas in respect to French cookery. Having heard
much of it, with no very distinct idea what it is, our
people have somehow fallen into the notion that its
forte lies in high spicing, — and so, when our cooks
put a great abundance of clove, mace, nutmeg, and
cinnamon into their preparations, they fancy that they
are growing up to be French cooks. But the fact is,
that the Americans and English are far more given
to spicing than the French. Spices in our made
dishes are abundant, and their taste is strongly pronounced. In living a year in France I forgot the
taste of nutmeg, clove, and allspice, which had met
me in so many dishes in America.

The thing may be briefly defined. The English
and Americans deal in *spices*, the French in *flavors*, —

flavors many and subtile, imitating often in their delicacy those subtile blendings which Nature produces
in high-flavored fruits. The recipes of our cookery-
books are most of them of English origin, coming
down from the times of our phlegmatic ancestors,
when the solid, burly, beefy growth of the foggy isl-
and required the heat of fiery condiments, and could
digest heavy sweets. Witness the national recipe for
plum-pudding, which may be rendered, — Take a
pound of every indigestible substance you can think
of, boil into a cannon-ball, and serve in flaming
brandy. So of the Christmas mince-pie and many
other national dishes. But in America, owing to our
brighter skies and more fervid climate, we have developed an acute, nervous delicacy of temperament
far more akin to that of France than of England.

Half of the recipes in our cook-books are mere
murder to such constitutions and stomachs as we
grow here. We require to ponder these things, and
think how we in our climate and under our circumstances ought to live, and in doing so, we may,
without accusation of foreign foppery, take some
leaves from many foreign books.

But Christopher has prosed long enough. I must
now read this to my wife, and see what she says.

12

XI.

OUR HOUSE.

OUR gallant Bob Stephens, into whose life-boat
our Marianne has been received, has lately
taken the mania of house-building into his head. Bob
is somewhat fastidious, difficult to please, fond of
domesticities and individualities; and such a man
never can fit himself into a house built by another,
and accordingly house-building has always been his
favorite mental recreation. During all his courtship
as much time was taken up in planning a future house
as if he had money to build one; and all Marianne's
patterns, and the backs of half their letters, were
scrawled with ground-plans and elevations. But lat-
terly this chronic disposition has been quickened into
an acute form by the falling-in of some few thousands
to their domestic treasury, — left as the sole re-
siduum of a painstaking old aunt, who took it into
her head to make a will in Bob's favor, leaving, among
other good things, a nice little bit of land in a rural
district half an hour's railroad-ride from Boston.

So now ground-plans thicken, and my wife is being

consulted morning, noon, and night; and I never come into the room without finding their heads close together over a paper, and hearing Bob expatiate on his favorite idea of a library. He appears to have got so far as this, that the ceiling is to be of carved oak, with ribs running to a boss over head, and finished mediævally with ultramarine blue and gilding, — and then away he goes sketching Gothic patterns of book-shelves which require only experienced carvers, and the wherewithal to pay them, to be the divinest things in the world.

Marianne is exercised about china-closets and pantries, and about a bedroom on the ground-floor, — for, like all other women of our days, she expects not to have strength enough to run up-stairs oftener than once or twice a week; and my wife, who is a native genius in this line, and has planned in her time dozens of houses for acquaintances, wherein they are at this moment living happily, goes over every day with her pencil and ruler the work of rearranging the plans, according as the ideas of the young couple veer and vary.

One day Bob is importuned to give two feet off from his library for a closet in the bedroom, — but resists like a Trojan. The next morning, being mollified by private domestic supplications, Bob yields, and my wife rubs out the lines of yesterday, two feet

come off the library, and a closet is constructed. But
now the parlor proves too narrow, — the parlor-wall
must be moved two feet into the hall. Bob declares
this will spoil the symmetry of the latter; and if there
is anything he wants, it is a wide, generous, ample hall
to step into when you open the front-door.

"Well, then," says Marianne, "let's put two feet
more into the width of the house."

"Can't on account of the expense, you see," says
Bob. "You see every additional foot of outside wall
necessitates so many more bricks, so much more flooring, so much more roofing, etc."

And my wife, with thoughtful brow, looks over the
plans, and considers how two feet more are to be got
into the parlor without moving any of the walls.

"I say," says Bob, bending over her shoulder,
"here, take your two feet in the parlor, and put two
more feet on to the other side of the hall-stairs";
and he dashes heavily with his pencil.

"O, Bob!" exclaims Marianne, "there are the
kitchen-pantries! you ruin them, — and no place for
the cellar-stairs!"

"Hang the pantries and cellar-stairs!" says Bob.
"Mother must find a place for them somewhere else.
I say the house must be roomy and cheerful, and pantries and those things may take care of themselves;
they can be put *somewhere* well enough. No fear

but you will find a place for them somewhere. What do you women always want such a great enormous kitchen for?"

"It is not any larger than is necessary," said my wife, thoughtfully; "nothing is gained by taking off from it."

"What if you should put it all down into a basement," suggests Bob, "and so get it all out of sight together?"

"Never if it can be helped," said my wife. "Basement-kitchens are necessary evils, only to be tolerated in cities where land is too dear to afford any other."

So goes the discussion till the trio agree to sleep over it. The next morning an inspiration visits my wife's pillow. She is up and seizes plans and paper, and before six o'clock has enlarged the parlor very cleverly, by throwing out a bow-window. So waxes and wanes the prospective house, innocently battered down and rebuilt with India-rubber and black-lead. Doors are cut out to-night, and walled up to-morrow; windows knocked out here and put in there, as some observer suggests possibilities of too much or too little draught. Now all seems finished, when, lo, a discovery! There is no fireplace nor stove-flue in my lady's bedroom, and can be none without moving the bathing-room. Pencil and India-rubber are busy again, and for a while the whole house seems to threaten to fall to pieces with the confusion of the moving; the bath-room wanders like a ghost, now invading a closet, now threatening the tranquillity of the parlor, till at last it is laid by some unheard-of calculations of my wife's, and sinks to rest in a place so much better that every body wonders it never was thought of before.

"Papa," said Jenny, "it appears to me people don't exactly know what they want when they build; why don't you write a paper on house-building?"

"I have thought of it," said I, with the air of a man called to settle some great reform. "It must be entirely because Christopher has not written that our young people and mamma are tangling themselves daily in webs which are untangled the next day."

"You see," said Jenny, "they have only just so much money, and they want everything they can think of under the sun. There's Bob been studying architectural antiquities, and nobody knows what, and sketching all sorts of curly-whorlies; and Marianne has her notions about a parlor and boudoir and china-closets and bedroom-closets; and Bob wants a baronial hall; and mamma stands out for linen-closets and bathing-rooms and all that; and so among them all it will just end in getting them head over ears in debt."

The thing struck me as not improbable.

"I don't know, Jenny, whether my writing an article is going to prevent all this; but as my time in the

'Atlantic' is coming round, I may as well write on what I am obliged to think of, and so I will give a paper on the subject to enliven our next evening's session."

So that evening, when Bob and Marianne had dropped in as usual, and while the customary work of drawing and rubbing-out was going on at Mrs. Crowfield's sofa, I produced my paper and read as follows : —

OUR HOUSE.

THERE is a place called " Our House," which everybody knows of. The sailor talks of it in his dreams at sea. The wounded soldier, turning in his uneasy hospital-bed, brightens at the word; it is like the dropping of cool water in the desert, like the touch of cool fingers on a burning brow. " Our house," he says feebly, and the light comes back into his dim eyes, — for all homely charities, all fond thoughts, all purities, all that man loves on earth or hopes for in heaven, rise with the word.

" Our house " may be in any style of architecture, low or high. It may be the brown old farm-house, with its tall well-sweep ; or the one-story gambrel-roofed cottage ; or the large, square, white house, with green blinds, under the wind-swung elms of a century ; or it may be the log-cabin of the wilderness, with its one

room, — still there is a spell in the memory of it beyond all conjurations.　Its stone and brick and mortar
are like no other; its very clapboards and shingles
are dear to us, powerful to bring back the memories
of early days, and all that is sacred in home-love.

"Papa is getting quite sentimental," whispered Jenny, loud enough for me to hear.　I shook my head at
her impressively, and went on undaunted.

There is no one fact of our human existence that
has a stronger influence upon us than the house we
dwell in, — especially that in which our earlier and
more impressible years are spent.　The building and
arrangement of a. house influence the health, the comfort, the morals, the religion.　There have been houses
built so devoid of all consideration for the occupants,
so rambling and hap-hazard in the disposal of rooms,
so sunless and cheerless and wholly without snugness
or privacy, as to make it seem impossible to live a
joyous, generous, rational, religious family-life in them.
There are, we shame to say, in our cities *things*
called houses, built and rented by people who walk
erect and have the general air and manner of civilized
and Christianized men, which are so inhuman in their
building that they can only be called snares and traps
for souls, — places where children cannot well escape

growing up filthy and impure, — places where to form a home is impossible, and to live a decent, Christian life would require miraculous strength.

A celebrated British philanthropist, who had devoted much study to the dwellings of the poor, gave it as his opinion that temperance-societies were a hopeless undertaking in London, unless these dwellings underwent a transformation. They were so squalid, so dark, so comfortless, so constantly pressing upon the senses foulness, pain, and inconvenience, that it was only by being drugged with gin and opium that their miserable inhabitants could find heart to drag on life from day to day. He had himself tried the experiment of reforming a drunkard by taking him from one of these loathsome dens, and enabling him to rent a tenement in a block of model lodging-houses which had been built under his supervision. The young man had been a designer of figures for prints; he was of a delicate frame, and a nervous, susceptible temperament. Shut in one miserable room with his wife and little children, without the possibility of pure air, with only filthy, fetid water to drink, with the noise of other miserable families resounding through the thin partitions, what possibility was there of doing anything except by the help of stimulants, which for a brief hour lifted him above the perception of these miseries? Changed at once to a neat flat, where, for

12*

the same rent as his former den, he had three good rooms, with water for drinking, house-service, and bathing freely supplied, and the blessed sunshine and air coming in through windows well arranged for ventilation, he became in a few weeks a new man. In the charms of the little spot which he could call home, its quiet, its order, his former talent came back to him, and he found strength, in pure air and pure water and those purer thoughts of which they are the emblems, to abandon burning and stupefying stimulants.

The influence of dwelling-houses for good or for evil — their influence on the brain, the nerves, and, through these, on the heart and life — is one of those things that cannot be enough pondered by those who build houses to sell or rent.

Something more generous ought to inspire a man than merely the percentage which he can get for his money. He who would build houses should think a little on the subject. He should reflect what houses are for, — what they may be made to do for human beings. The great majority of houses in cities are not built by the indwellers themselves, — they are built *for* them by those who invest their money in this way, with little other thought than the percentage which the investment will return.

For persons of ample fortune there are, indeed, palatial residences, with all that wealth can do to render life delightful. But in that class of houses which must be the lot of the large majority, those which must be chosen by young men in the beginning of life, when means are comparatively restricted, there is yet wide room for thought and the judicious application of money.

In looking over houses to be rented by persons of moderate means, one cannot help longing to build, — one sees so many ways in which the same sum which built an inconvenient and unpleasant house might have been made to build a delightful one.

"That's so!" said Bob, with emphasis. "Don't you remember, Marianne, how many dismal, commonplace, shabby houses we trailed through?"

"Yes," said Marianne. "You remember those houses with such little squeezed rooms and that flourishing staircase, with the colored-glass china-closet window, and no butler's sink?"

"Yes," said Bob; "and those astonishing, abominable stone abortions that adorned the door-steps. People do lay out a deal of money to make houses look ugly, it must be confessed."

"One would willingly," said Marianne, "dispense with frightful stone ornaments in front, and with heavy mouldings inside, which are of no possible use or beauty, and with showy plaster cornices and centre-pieces in the parlor-ceilings, and even with marble mantels, for the luxury of hot and cold water in each chamber, and a couple of comfortable bath-rooms. Then, the disposition of windows and doors is so wholly without regard to convenience! How often we find rooms, meant for bedrooms, where really there is no good place for either bed or dressing-table!"

Here my wife looked up, having just finished re-drawing the plans to the latest alteration.

"One of the greatest reforms that could be, in these reforming days," she observed, "would be to have women architects. The mischief with houses built to rent is that they are all mere male contrivances. No woman would ever plan chambers where there is no earthly place to set a bed except against a window or door, or waste the room in entries that might be made into closets. I don't see, for my part, *apropos* to the modern movement for opening new professions to the female sex, why there should not be well-educated female architects. The planning and arrangement of houses, and the laying-out of grounds, are a fair subject of womanly knowledge and taste. It is the teaching of Nature. What would anybody think of a bluebird's nest that had been built entirely by Mr. Blue, without the help of his wife?"

"My dear," said I, "you must positively send a paper on this subject to the next Woman's-Rights Convention."

"I am of Sojourner Truth's opinion," said my wife, — "that the best way to prove the propriety of one's doing anything is to go and *do it*. A woman who should have energy to go through the preparatory studies and set to work in this field would, I am sure, soon find employment."

"If she did as well as you would do, my dear," said I. "There are plenty of young women in our Boston high-schools who are going through higher fields of mathematics than are required by the architect, and the schools for design show the flexibility and fertility of the female pencil. The thing appears to me altogether more feasible than many other openings which have been suggested to woman."

"Well," said Jenny, "is n't papa ever to go on with his paper?"

I continued : —

What ought "our house" to be? Could any other question be asked admitting in its details of such varied answers, — answers various as the means, the character, and situation of different individuals? But there are great wants pertaining to every human being, into which all lesser ones run. There are things in a house that every one, high or low, rich or poor, ought, according to his means, to seek. I think I shall class them according to the elemental division of the old philosophers, — Fire, Air, Earth, and Water. These form the groundwork of this *need-be*, — the *sine-qua-nons* of a house.

"Fire, air, earth, and water! I don't understand," said Jenny.

"Wait a little till you do, then," said I. "I will try to make my meaning plain."

The first object of a house is shelter from the elements. This object is effected by a tent or wigwam which keeps off rain and wind. The first disadvantage of this shelter is, that the vital air which you take into your lungs, and on the purity of which depends the purity of blood and brain and nerve, is vitiated. In the wigwam or tent you are constantly taking in poison, more or less active, with every inspiration. Napoleon had his army sleep without tents. He stated, that from experience, he found it more healthy; and wonderful have been the instances of delicate persons gaining constantly in vigor from being obliged, in the midst of hardships, to sleep constantly in the open air. Now the first problem in house-building is to combine the advantage of shelter with the fresh elasticity of out-door air. I am not going to give here a treatise on ventilation, but merely to say, in general terms, that the first object of a house-builder or contriver should be to make a healthy house ; and the first requisite of a healthy house is a pure, sweet, elastic air.

I am in favor, therefore, of those plans of house-building which have wide central spaces, whether halls or courts, into which all the rooms open, and which necessarily preserve a body of fresh air for the use of them all. In hot climates this is the object of the central court which cuts into the body of the house, with its fountain and flowers, and its galleries, into which the various apartments open. When people are restricted for space, and cannot afford to give up wide central portions of the house for the mere purposes of passage, this central hall can be made a pleasant sitting-room. With tables, chairs, book-cases, and sofas comfortably disposed, this ample central room above and below is, in many respects, the most agreeable lounging-room of the house ; while the parlors below and the chambers above, opening upon it, form agreeable withdrawing-rooms for purposes of greater privacy.

It is customary with many persons to sleep with bedroom windows open, — a very imperfect and often dangerous mode of procuring that supply of fresh air which a sleeping-room requires. In a house constructed in the manner indicated, windows might be freely left open in these central halls, producing there a constant movement of air, and the doors of the bedrooms placed ajar, when a very slight opening in the windows would create a free circulation through the apartments.

In the planning of a house, thought should be had as to the general disposition of the windows, and the quarters from which favoring breezes may be expected should be carefully considered. Windows should be so arranged that draughts of air can be thrown quite through and across the house. . How often have we seen pale mothers and drooping babes fanning and panting during some of our hot days on the sunny side of a house, while the breeze that should have cooled them beat in vain against a dead wall ! One longs sometimes to knock holes through partitions, and let in the air of heaven.

No other gift of God, so precious, so inspiring, is treated with such utter irreverence and contempt in the calculations of us mortals as this same air of heaven. A sermon on oxygen, if one had a preacher who understood the subject, might do more to repress sin than the most orthodox discourse to show when and how and why sin came. A minister gets up in a crowded lecture-room, where the mephitic air almost makes the candles burn blue, and bewails the deadness of the church, — the church the while, drugged by the poisoned air, growing sleepier and sleepier, though they feel dreadfully wicked for being so.

Little Jim, who, fresh from his afternoon's ramble in the fields, last evening said his prayers dutifully, and lay down to sleep in a most Christian frame, this morning sits up in bed with his hair bristling with crossness, strikes at his nurse, and declares he won't say his prayers, — that he don't want to be good. The simple difference is, that the child, having slept in a close box of a room, his brain all night fed by poison, is in a mild state of moral insanity. Delicate women remark that it takes them till eleven or twelve o'clock to get up their strength in the morning. Query, — Do they sleep with closed windows and doors, and with heavy bed-curtains?

The houses built by our ancestors were better ventilated in certain respects than modern ones, with all their improvements. The great central chimney, with its open fireplaces in the different rooms, created a constant current which carried off foul and vitiated air. In these days, how common is it to provide rooms with only a flue for a stove! This flue is kept shut in summer, and in winter opened only to admit a close stove, which burns away the vital portion of the air quite as fast as the occupants breathe it away. The sealing-up of fireplaces and introduction of air-tight stoves may, doubtless, be a saving of fuel: it saves, too, more than that; in thousands and thousands of cases it has saved people from all further human wants, and put an end forever to any needs short of the six feet of narrow earth which are man's only inalienable property. In other words, since the invention of air-tight stoves, thousands have died of slow poison. It is a terrible thing to reflect upon, that our northern winters last from November to May, six long months, in which many families confine themselves to one room, of which every window-crack has been carefully calked to make it air-tight, where an air-tight stove keeps the atmosphere at a temperature between eighty and ninety, and the inmates sitting there with all their winter clothes on become enervated both by the heat and by the poisoned air, for which there is no escape but the occasional opening of a door.

It is no wonder that the first result of all this is such a delicacy of skin and lungs that about half the inmates are obliged to give up going into the open air during the six cold months, because they invariably catch cold, if they do so. It is no wonder that the cold caught about the first of December has by the first of March become a fixed consumption, and that the opening of the spring, which ought to bring life and health, in so many cases brings death.

We hear of the lean condition in which the poor bears emerge from their six-months' wintering, during which they subsist on the fat which they have acquired the previous summer. Even so in our long winters, multitudes of delicate people subsist on the daily waning strength which they acquired in the season when windows and doors were open, and fresh air was a constant luxury. No wonder we hear of spring fever and spring biliousness, and have thousands of nostrums for clearing the blood in the spring. All these things are the pantings and palpitations of a system run down under slow poison, unable to get a step farther. Better, far better, the old houses of the olden time, with their great roaring fires, and their bedrooms where the snow came in and the wintry winds whistled. Then, to be sure, you froze your back while you burned your face, your water froze nightly in your pitcher, your breath congealed in ice-wreaths on the blankets, and you could write your name on the pretty snow-wreath that had sifted in through the window-cracks. But you woke full of life and vigor, — you looked out into whirling snow-storms without a shiver, and thought nothing of plunging through drifts as high as your head on your daily way to school. You jingled in sleighs, you snowballed, you lived in snow like a snow-bird, and your blood coursed and tingled, in full tide of good, merry, real life, through your veins, — none of the slow-creeping, black blood which clogs the brain and lies like a weight on the vital wheels!

"Mercy upon us, papa!" said Jenny, "I hope we need not go back to such houses!"

"No, my dear," I replied. "I only said that such houses were better than those which are all winter closed by double windows and burnt-out air-tight stoves."

The perfect house is one in which there is a constant escape of every foul and vitiated particle of air through one opening, while a constant supply of fresh out-door air is admitted by another. In winter, this out-door air must pass through some process by which it is brought up to a temperate warmth.

Take a single room, and suppose on one side a current of out-door air which has been warmed by passing through the air-chamber of a modern furnace. Its temperature need not be above sixty-five, — it answers breathing purposes better at that. On the other side of the room let there be an open wood- or coal-fire. One cannot conceive the purposes of warmth and ventilation more perfectly combined.

Suppose a house with a great central hall, into which a current of fresh, temperately warmed air is continually pouring. Each chamber opening upon this hall has a chimney up whose flue the rarefied air is constantly passing, drawing up with it all the foul and poisonous gases. That house is well ventilated, and in a way that need bring no dangerous draughts upon the most delicate invalid. For the better securing of privacy in sleeping-rooms, we have seen two doors employed, one of which is made with slats, like a window-blind, so that air is freely transmitted without exposing the interior.

When we speak of fresh air, we insist on the full rigor of the term. It must not be the air of a cellar, heavily laden with the poisonous nitrogen of turnips and cabbages, but good, fresh, out-door air from a cold-air pipe, so placed as not to get the lower stratum near the ground, where heavy damps and exhalations collect, but high up, in just the clearest and most elastic region.

The conclusion of the whole matter is, that as all of man's and woman's peace and comfort, all their love, all their amiability, all their religion, have got to come to them, while they live in this world, through the medium of the brain, — and as black, uncleansed blood acts on the brain as a poison, and as no other than black, uncleansed blood can be got by the lungs out of impure air, — the first object of the man who builds a house is to secure a pure and healthy atmosphere therein.

Therefore, in allotting expenses, set this down as a *must-be:* " Our house must have fresh air, — everywhere, 'at all times, winter and summer." Whether we have stone facings or no, —whether our parlor has cornices or marble mantles or no, — whether our doors are machine-made or hand-made. All our fixtures shall be of the plainest and simplest, but we will have fresh air. We will open our door with a latch and string, if we cannot afford lock and knob and fresh air too, — but in our house we will live cleanly and Christianly. We will no more breathe the foul air rejected from a neighbor's lungs than we will use a neighbor's tooth-brush and hair-brush. Such is the first essential of "our house," — the first great element of human health and happiness, — AIR.

"I say, Marianne," said Bob, "have we got fireplaces in our chambers?"

"Mamma took care of that," said Marianne.

"You may be quite sure," said I, "if your mother has had a hand in planning your house, that the ventilation is cared for."

It must be confessed that Bob's principal idea in a house had been a Gothic library, and his mind had labored more on the possibility of adapting some favorite bits from the baronial antiquities to modern needs than on anything so terrestrial as air. Therefore he awoke as from a dream, and taking two or three monstrous inhalations, he seized the plans and began looking over them with new energy. Meanwhile I went on with my prelection.

The second great vital element for which provision must be made in "our house" is FIRE. By which I do not mean merely artificial fire, but fire in all its extent and branches, — the heavenly fire which God sends us daily on the bright wings of sunbeams, as well as the mimic fires by which we warm our dwellings, cook our food, and light our nightly darkness.

To begin, then, with heavenly fire or sunshine. If God's gift of vital air is neglected and undervalued, His gift of sunshine appears to be hated. There are many houses where not a cent has been expended on ventilation, but where hundreds of dollars have been freely lavished to keep out the sunshine. The chamber, truly, is tight as a box, — it has no fireplace, not even a ventilator opening into the stove-flue ; but, oh, joy and gladness ! it has outside blinds and inside folding-shutters, so that in the brightest of days we may create there a darkness that may be felt. To observe the generality of New-England houses, a spectator might imagine they were planned for the torrid zone, where the great object is to keep out a furnace-draught of burning air.

But let us look over the months of our calendar. In which of them do we not need fires on our hearths ?

We will venture to say that from October to June all families, whether they actually have it or not, would be the more comfortable for a morning and evening fire. For eight months in the year the weather varies on the scale of cool, cold, colder, and freezing ; and for all the four other months what is the number of days that really require the torrid-zone system of shutting up houses? We all know that extreme heat is the exception, and not the rule.

Yet let anybody travel, as I did last year, through the valley of the Connecticut, and observe the houses. All clean and white and neat and well-to-do, with their turfy yards and their breezy great elms, — but all shut up from basement to attic, as if the inmates had all sold out and gone to China. Not a window-blind open above or below. Is the house inhabited? No, — yes, — there is a faint stream of blue smoke from the kitchen-chimney, and half a window-blind open in some distant back-part of the house. They are living there in the dim shadows, bleaching like potato-sprouts in the cellar.

"I can tell you why they do it, papa," said Jenny, — "It's the flies, and flies are certainly worthy to be one of the plagues of Egypt. I can't myself blame people that shut up their rooms and darken their houses in fly-time, — do you, mamma?"

"Not in extreme cases; though I think there is but a short season when this is necessary; yet the habit of shutting up lasts the year round, and gives to New-England villages that dead, silent, cold, uninhabited look which is so peculiar.

"The one fact that a traveller would gather in passing through our villages would be this," said I, "that the people live in their houses and in the dark. Rarely do you see doors and windows open, people sitting at them, chairs in the yard, and signs that the inhabitants are living out-of-doors."

"Well," said Jenny, "I have told you why, for I have been at Uncle Peter's in summer, and aunt does her spring-cleaning in May, and then she shuts all the blinds and drops all the curtains, and the house stays clean till October. That's the whole of it. If she had all her windows open, there would be paint and windows to be cleaned every week; and who is to do it? For my part, I can't much blame her."

"Well," said I, "I have my doubts about the sovereign efficacy of living in the dark, even if the great object of existence were to be rid of flies. I remember, during this same journey, stopping for a day or two at a country boarding-house which was dark as Egypt from cellar to garret. The long, dim, gloomy dining-room was first closed by outside blinds, and then by impenetrable paper curtains, notwithstanding which it swarmed and buzzed like a beehive. You found where the cake-plate was by the buzz which your hand made, if you chanced to reach in that direction. It was disagreeable, because in the darkness flies could not always be distinguished from huckleberries ; and I could n't help wishing, that, since we must have the flies, we might at last have the light and air to console us under them. People darken their rooms and shut up every avenue of out-door enjoyment, and sit and think of nothing but flies ; in fact, flies are all they have left. No wonder they become morbid on the subject."

"Well, now, papa talks just like a man, doesn't he ?" said Jenny. "He has n't the responsibility of keeping things clean. I wonder what he would do, if he were a housekeeper."

"Do ? I will tell you. I would do the best I could. I would shut my eyes on fly-specks, and open them on the beauties of Nature. I would let the cheerful sun in all day long, in all but the few summer days when coolness is the one thing needful : those days may be soon numbered every year. I would make a calculation in the spring how much it would cost to hire a woman to keep my windows and paint clean, and I would do with one less gown and have her ; and when I had spent all I could afford on cleaning windows and paint, I would harden my heart and turn off my eyes, and enjoy my sunshine, and my fresh air, my breezes, and all that can be seen through the picture-windows of an open, airy house, and snap my fingers at the flies. There you have it." .

"Papa's hobby is sunshine," said Marianne.

"Why shouldn't it be? Was God mistaken, when He made the sun? Did He make him for us to hold a life's battle with? Is that vital power which reddens the cheek of the peach and pours sweetness through the fruits and flowers of no use to us? Look at plants that grow without sun, — wan, pale, long-visaged, holding feeble, imploring hands of supplication towards the light. Can human beings afford to throw away a vitalizing force so pungent, so exhilarating? You remember the experiment of a prison, where one row of cells had daily sunshine, and the others none. With the same regimen, the same cleanliness, the same care, the inmates of the sunless cells were visited with sickness and death in double measure. Our whole population in New England are groaning and suffering under afflictions, the result of a depressed vitality, — neuralgia, with a new ache for every day of the year, rheumatism, consumption, general debility; for all these a thousand nostrums are daily advertised, and money enough is spent on them to equip an army, while we are fighting against, wasting, and throwing away with both hands that blessed influence which comes nearest to pure vitality of anything God has given.

"Who is it that the Bible describes as a sun, arising with healing in his wings? Surely, that sunshine which is the chosen type and image of His love must be healing through all the recesses of our daily life, drying damp and mould, defending from moth and rust, sweetening ill smells, clearing from the nerves the vapors of melancholy, making life cheery. If I did not know Him, I should certainly adore and worship the sun, the most blessed and beautiful image of Him among things visible! In the land of Egypt, in the day of God's wrath, there was darkness, but in the land of Goshen there was light. I am a Goshenite, and mean to walk in the light, and forswear the works of darkness. But to proceed with our reading."

"Our house" shall be set on a southeast line, so that there shall not be a sunless room in it, and windows shall be so arranged that it can be traversed and transpierced through and through with those bright shafts of light which come straight from God.

"Our house" shall not be blockaded with a dank, dripping mass of shrubbery set plumb against the windows, keeping out light and air. There shall be room all round it for breezes to sweep, and sunshine to sweeten and dry and vivify; and I would warn all good souls who begin life by setting out two little ever-green-trees within a foot of each of their front-windows, that these trees will grow and increase till their front-rooms will be brooded over by a sombre, stifling shadow fit only for ravens to croak in.

One would think, by the way some people hasten to convert a very narrow front-yard into a dismal jungle, that the only danger of our New England climate was sunstroke. Ah, in those drizzling months which form at least one half of our life here, what sullen, censo-rious, uncomfortable, unhealthy thoughts are bred of living in dark, chilly rooms, behind such dripping thickets? Our neighbors' faults assume a deeper hue, —life seems a dismal thing, — our very religion grows mouldy.

My idea of a house is, that, as far as is consistent with shelter and reasonable privacy, it should give you on first entering an open, breezy, out-door freshness of sensation. Every window should be a picture; sun and trees and clouds and green grass should seem never to be far from us. "Our house" may shade but not darken us. "Our house" shall have bow-windows, many, sunny, and airy, — not for the purpose of being cleaned and shut up, but to be open and enjoyed. There shall be long verandahs above and below, where invalids may walk dry-shod, and enjoy open-air recre-ation in wettest weather. In short, I will try to have "our house" combine as far as possible the sunny, joyous, fresh life of a gypsy in the fields and woods with the quiet and neatness and comfort and shelter of a roof, rooms, floors, and carpets.

After heavenly fire, I have a word to say of earthly, artificial fires. Furnaces, whether of hot water, steam, or hot air, are all healthy and admirable provisions for warming our houses during the eight or nine months of our year that we must have artificial heat, if only, as I have said, fireplaces keep up a current of ventilation.

The kitchen-range with its water-back I humbly salute. It is a great throbbing heart, and sends its warm tides of cleansing, comforting fluid all through the house. One could wish that this friendly dragon could be in some way moderated in his appetite for coal, — he does consume without mercy, it must be confessed, — but then great is the work he has to do. At any hour of day or night, in the most distant part of your house, you have but to turn a stop-cock and your red dragon sends you hot water for your needs; your washing-day becomes a mere play-day; your pantry has its ever-ready supply; and then, by a little judicious care in arranging apartments and economizing heat, a range may make two or three chambers comfortable in winter weather. A range with a water-back is among the *must-bes* in "our house."

Then, as to the evening light, — I know nothing as yet better than gas, where it can be had. I would certainly not have a house without it. The great objection to it is the danger of its escape through imperfect fixtures. But it must not do this ; a fluid that kills a tree or a plant with one breath must certainly be a dangerous ingredient in the atmosphere, and if admitted into houses, must be introduced with every safeguard.

There are families living in the country who make their own gas by a very simple process. This is worth an inquiry from those who build. There are also contrivances now advertised, with good testimonials, of domestic machines for generating gas, said to be perfectly safe, simple to be managed, and producing a light superior to that of the city gas-works. This also is worth an inquiry when " our house" is to be in the country.

And now I come to the next great vital element for which " our house" must provide, — WATER. " Water, water, everywhere," — it must be plentiful, it must be easy to get at, it must be pure. Our ancestors had some excellent ideas in home-living and house-building. Their houses were, generally speaking, very sensibly contrived, — roomy, airy, and comfortable ; but in their water-arrangements they had little mercy on

womankind.   The well was out in the yard ; and in
winter one must flounder through snow and bring up
the ice-bound bucket, before one could fill the tea-
kettle for breakfast.   For a sovereign princess of the
republic this was hardly respectful or respectable.
Wells have come somewhat nearer in modern times ;
but the idea of a constant supply of fresh water by the
simple turning of a stop-cock has not yet visited the
great body of our houses.   Were we free to build
" our house " just as we wish it, there should be a
bath-room to every two or three inmates, and the hot
and cold water should circulate to every chamber.

Among our *must-bes*, we would lay by a generous
sum for plumbing.   Let us have our bath-rooms, and
our arrangements for cleanliness and health in kitchen
and pantry ; and afterwards let the quality of our
lumber and the style of our finishings be according to
the sum we have left.   The power to command a
warm bath in a house at any hour of day or night is
better in bringing up a family of children than any
amount of ready medicine.   In three-quarters of
childish ailments the warm bath is an almost immediate remedy.   Bad colds, incipient fevers, rheu-
matisms, convulsions, neuralgias innumerable, are
washed off in their first beginnings, and run down the
lead pipes into oblivion.   Have, then, O friend, all
the water in your house that you can afford, and en-·

large your ideas of the worth of it, that you *may* afford a great deal. A bathing-room is nothing to you that requires an hour of lifting and fire-making to prepare it for use. The apparatus is too cumbrous, — you do not turn to it. But when your chamber opens upon a neat, quiet little nook, and you have only to turn your stop-cocks and all is ready, your remedy is at hand, you use it constantly. You are waked in the night by a scream, and find little Tom sitting up, wild with burning fever. In three minutes he is in the bath, quieted and comfortable; you get him back, cooled and tranquil, to his little crib, and in the morning he wakes as if nothing had happened.

Why should not so invaluable and simple a remedy for disease, such a preservative of health, such a comfort, such a stimulus, be considered as much a matter-ter-of-course in a house as a kitchen-chimney? At least there should be one bath-room always in order, so arranged that all the family can have access to it, if one cannot afford the luxury of many.

A house in which water is universally and skilfully distributed is so much easier to take care of as almost to verify the' saying of a friend, that his house was so contrived that it did its own work : one had better do without carpets on the floors, without stuffed sofas and rocking-chairs, and secure this.

13*

"Well, papa," said Marianne, "you have made out all your four elements in your house, except one. I can't imagine what you want of *earth*."

"I thought," said Jenny, "that the less of our common mother we had in our houses, the better housekeepers we were."

"My dears," said I, "we philosophers must give an occasional dip into the mystical, and say something apparently absurd for the purpose of explaining that we mean nothing in particular by it. It gives common people an idea of our sagacity, to find how clear we come out of our apparent contradictions and absurdities. Listen."

For the fourth requisite of "our house," EARTH, let me point you to your mother's plant-window, and beg you to remember the fact that through our long, dreary winters we are never a month without flowers, and the vivid interest which always attaches to growing things. The perfect house, as I conceive it, is to combine as many of the advantages of living out of doors as may be consistent with warmth and shelter, and one of these is the sympathy with green and growing things. Plants are nearer in their relations to human health and vigor than is often imagined. The cheerfulness that well-kept plants impart to a room comes not merely from gratification of the eye, — there is a healthful exhalation from them, they are a corrective of the impurities of the atmosphere. Plants, too, are valuable as tests of the vitality of the atmosphere; their drooping and failure convey to us information that something is amiss with it. A lady once told me that she could never raise plants in her parlors on account of the gas and anthracite coal. I answered, "Are you not afraid to live and bring up your children in an atmosphere which blights your plants?" If the gas escapes from the pipes, and the red-hot anthracite coal or the red-hot air-tight stove burns out all the vital part of the air, so that healthy plants in a few days wither and begin to drop their leaves, it is a sign that the air must be looked to and reformed. It is a fatal augury for a room that plants cannot be made to thrive in it. Plants should not turn pale, be long-jointed, long-leaved, and spindling; and where they grow in this way, we may be certain that there is a want of vitality for human beings. But where plants appear as they do in the open air, with vigorous, stocky growth, and short-stemmed, deep-green leaves, we may believe the conditions of that atmosphere are healthy for human lungs.

It is pleasant to see how the custom of plant-growing has spread through our country. In how many farm-house windows do we see petunias and nasturtiums vivid with bloom while snows are whirling with-

out, and how much brightness have those cheap en-
joyments shed on the lives of those who cared for
them! We do not believe there is a human being
who would not become a passionate lover of plants,
if circumstances once made it imperative to tend upon
and watch the growth of one. The history of Picciola
for substance has been lived over and over by many
a man and woman who once did not know that there
was a particle of plant-love in their souls. But to the
proper care of plants in pots there are many hin-
drances and drawbacks. The dust chokes the little
pores of their green lungs, and they require constant
showering; and to carry all one's plants to a sink or
porch for this purpose is a labor which many will not
endure. Consequently plants often do not get a showering once a month! We should try to imitate more
closely the action of Mother Nature, who washes
every green child of hers nightly with dews, which lie
glittering on its leaves till morning.

"Yes, there it is!" said Jenny. "I think I could
manage with plants, if it were not for this eternal
showering and washing they seem to require to keep
them fresh. They are always tempting one to spatter
the carpet and surrounding furniture, which are not
equally benefited by the libation."

"It is partly for that very reason," I replied, "that

the plan of 'our house' provides for the introduction of Mother Earth, as you will see."

A perfect house, according to my idea, should always include in it a little compartment where plants can be kept, can be watered, can be defended from the dust, and have the sunshine and all the conditions of growth.

People have generally supposed a conservatory to be one of the last trappings of wealth, — something not to be thought of for those in modest circumstances. But is this so? You have a bow-window in your parlor. Leave out the flooring, fill the space with rich earth, close it from the parlor by glass doors, and you have room for enough plants and flowers to keep you gay and happy all winter. If on the south side, where the sunbeams have power, it requires no heat but that which warms the parlor; and the comfort of it is incalculable, and the expense a mere trifle greater than that of the bow-window alone.

In larger houses a larger space might be appropriated in this way. We will not call it a conservatory, because that name suggests ideas of gardeners, and mysteries of culture and rare plants, which bring all sorts of care and expense in their train. We would rather call it a greenery, a room floored with earth, with glass sides to admit the sun, — and let it open on as many other rooms of the house as possible.

Why should not the dining-room and parlor be all winter connected by a spot of green and flowers, with plants, mosses, and ferns for the shadowy portions, and such simple blooms as petunias and nasturtiums garlanding the sunny portion near the windows? If near the water-works, this greenery might be enlivened by the play of a fountain, whose constant spray would give that softness to the air which is so often burned away by the dry heat of the furnace.

"And do you really think, papa, that houses built in this way are a practical result to be aimed at?" said Jenny. "To me it seems like a dream of the Alhambra."

"Yet I happen to have seen real people in our day living in just such a house," said I. "I could point you, this very hour, to a cottage, which in style of building is the plainest possible, which unites many of the best ideas of a true house. My dear, can you sketch the ground plan of that house we saw in Brighton?"

"Here it is," said my wife, after a few dashes with her pencil, — "an inexpensive house, yet one of the pleasantest I ever saw."

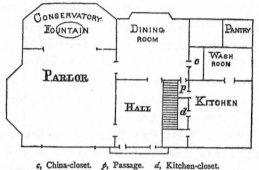

c, China-closet. *p*, Passage. *d*, Kitchen-closet.

"This cottage, which might, at the rate of prices before the war, have been built for five thousand dollars, has many of the requirements which I seek for a house. It has two stories, and a tier of very pleasant attic-rooms, two bathing-rooms, and the water carried into each story. The parlor and dining-room both look into a little bower, where a fountain is ever playing into a little marble basin, and which all the year through has its green and bloom. It is heated simply from the furnace by a register, like any other room of the house, and requires no more care than a delicate woman could easily give. The brightness and cheerfulness it brings during our long, dreary winters is incredible."

But one caution is necessary in all such appendages. The earth must be thorougly underdrained to prevent the vapors of stagnant water, and have a large admixture of broken charcoal to obviate the consequences of vegetable decomposition. Great care must be taken that there be no leaves left to fall and decay on the ground, since vegetable exhalations poison the air. With these precautions such a plot will soften and purify the air of a house.

Where the means do not allow even so small a conservatory, a recessed window might be fitted with a deep box, which should have a drain-pipe at the bottom, and a thick layer of broken charcoal and gravel, with a mixture of fine wood-soil and sand, for the top stratum. Here ivies may be planted, which will run and twine and strike their little tendrils here and there, and give the room in time the aspect of a bower; the various greenhouse nasturtiums will make winter gorgeous with blossoms. In windows unblest by sunshine — and, alas, such are many! — one can cultivate ferns and mosses; the winter-growing ferns, of which there are many varieties, can be mixed with mosses and woodland flowers.

Early in February, when the cheerless frosts of winter seem most wearisome, the common blue violet, woodanemone, hepatica, or rock-columbine, if planted in this way, will begin to bloom. The common partridgeberry, with its brilliant scarlet fruit and dark green leaves, will also grow finely in such situations, and have a beautiful effect. These things require daily showering to keep them fresh, and the moisture arising from them will soften and freshen the too dry air of heated winter rooms.

Thus I have been through my four essential elements in house-building, — air, fire, water, and earth. I would provide for these before anything else. After they are secured, I would gratify my taste and fancy as far as possible in other ways. I quite agree with Bob in hating commonplace houses, and longing for some little bit of architectural effect; and I grieve profoundly that every step in that direction must cost so much. I have also a taste for niceness of finish. I have no objection to silver-plated door-locks and hinges, none to windows which are an entire plate of clear glass. I congratulate neighbors who are so fortunate as to be able to get them; and after I have put all the essentials into a house, I would have these too, if I had the means.

But if all my wood-work were to be without groove or moulding, if my mantels were to be of simple wood, if my doors were all to be machine-made, and my lumber of the second quality, I would have my bath-rooms, my conservatory, my sunny bow-windows, and my perfect ventilation; and my house would then be so pleasant, and every one in it in such a cheerful mood, that it would verily seem to be ceiled with cedar.

Speaking of ceiling with cedar, I have one thing more to say. We Americans have a country abounding in beautiful timber, of whose beauties we know nothing, on account of the pernicious and stupid habit of covering it with white paint.

The celebrated zebra-wood with its golden stripes cannot exceed in quaint beauty the grain of unpainted chestnut, prepared simply with a coat or two of oil. The butternut has a rich golden brown, the very darling color of painters, — a shade so rich, and grain so beautiful, that it is of itself as charming to look at as a rich picture. The black-walnut, with its heavy depth of tone, works in well as an adjunct; and as to oak, what can we say enough of its quaint and many shadings? Even common pine, which has been considered not decent to look upon till hastily shrouded in a friendly blanket of white paint, has, when oiled and varnished, the beauty of satin-wood. The second quality of pine, which has what are called *shakes* in it, under this mode of treatment often shows clouds and veins equal in beauty to the choicest woods. The cost of such a finish is greatly less than that of the old method; and it saves those days and weeks of cleaning which are demanded by white paint, while its general tone is softer and more harmonious. Experiments in color may be tried in the combination of these woods, which at small expense produce the most charming effects.

As to paper-hangings, we are proud to say that our American manufacturers now furnish all that can be desired. There are some branches of design where artistic, ingenious France must still excel us ; but whoso has a house to fit up, let him first look at what his own country has to show, and he will be astonished.

There is one topic in house-building on which I would add a few words. The difficulty of procuring and keeping good servants, which must long be one of our chief domestic troubles, warns us so to arrange our houses that we shall need as few as possible. There is the greatest conceivable difference in the planning and building of houses as to the amount of work which will be necessary to keep them in respectable condition. Some houses require a perfect staff of house-maids ; — there are plated hinges to be rubbed, paint to be cleaned, with intricacies of moulding and carving which daily consume hours of dusting to preserve them from a slovenly look. Simple finish, unpainted wood, a general distribution of water through the dwelling, will enable a very large house to be cared for by one pair of hands, and yet maintain a creditable appearance.

In kitchens one servant may perform the work of two by a close packing of all the conveniences for cooking and such arrangements as shall save time and steps. Washing-day may be divested of its terrors by suitable provisions for water, hot and cold, by wringers, which save at once the strength of the linen and of the laundress, and by drying-closets connected with ranges, where articles can in a few moments be perfectly dried. These, with the use of a small mangle, such as is now common in America, reduce the labors of the laundry one half.

There are many more things which might be said of "our house," and Christopher may, perhaps, find some other opportunity to say them. For the present his pen is tired and ceaseth.

XII.

HOME RELIGION.

IT was Sunday evening, and our little circle were convened by my study-fireside, where a crackling hickory fire proclaimed the fall of the year to be coming on, and cold weather impending. Sunday evenings, my married boys and girls are fond of coming home and gathering round the old hearthstone, and "making believe" that they are children again. We get out the old-fashioned music-books, and sing old hymns to very old tunes, and my wife and her matron daughters talk about the babies in the intervals; and we discourse of the sermon, and of the choir, and all the general outworks of good pious things which Sunday suggests.

"Papa," said Marianne, "you are closing up your House and Home Papers, are you not?"

"Yes, — I am come to the last one, for this year at least."

"My dear," said my wife, "there is one subject you have n't touched on yet; you ought not to close the year without it; no house and home can be complete without Religion : you should write a paper on Home Religion."

My wife, as you may have seen in these papers, is an old-fashioned woman, something of a conservative. I am, I confess, rather given to progress and speculation; but I feel always as if I were going on in these ways with a string round my waist, and my wife's hand steadily pulling me back into the old paths. My wife is a steady, Bible-reading, Sabbath-keeping woman, cherishing the memory of her fathers, and loving to do as they did, — believing, for the most part, that the paths well beaten by righteous feet are safest, even though much walking therein has worn away the grass and flowers. Nevertheless, she has an indulgent ear for all that gives promise of bettering anybody or anything, and therefore is not severe on any new methods that may arise in our progressive days of accomplishing old good objects.

"There must be a home religion," said my wife.

" I believe in home religion," said Bob Stephens, — "but not in the outward show of it. The best sort of religion is that which one keeps at the bottom of his heart, and which goes up thence quietly through all his actions, and not the kind that comes through a certain routine of forms and ceremonies. Do you suppose family prayers, now, and a blessing at meals, make people any better?"

"Depend upon it, Robert," said my wife, — she always calls him Robert on Sunday evenings, — " depend upon it, we are not so very much wiser than our fathers were, that we need depart from their good old ways. Of course I would have religion in the heart, and spreading quietly through the life; but does this interfere with those outward, daily acts of respect and duty which we owe to our Creator? It is too much the slang of our day to decry forms, and to exalt the excellency of the spirit in opposition to them; but tell me, are you satisfied with friendship that has none of the outward forms of friendship, or love that has none of the outward forms of love? Are you satisfied of the existence of a sentiment that has no outward mode of expression? Even the old heathen had their pieties; they would not begin a feast without a libation to their divinities, and there was a shrine in every well-regulated house for household gods."

"The trouble with all these things," said Bob, "is that they get to be mere forms. I never could see that family worship amounted to much more in most families."

"The outward expression of all good things is apt to degenerate into mere form," said I. "The outward expression of social good feeling becomes a mere form; but for that reason must we meet each other like oxen? not say, 'Good morning,' or 'Good evening,' or 'I am happy to see you'? Must we never use any of the forms of mutual good-will, except in those moments when we are excited by a real, present emotion? What would become of society? Forms are, so to speak, a daguerrotype of a past good feeling, meant to take and keep the impression of it when it is gone. Our best and most inspired moments are crystallized in them; and even when the spirit that created them is gone, they help to bring it back. Every one must be conscious that the use of the forms of social benevolence, even towards those who are personally unpleasant to us, tends to ameliorate prejudices. We see a man entering our door who is a weary bore, but we use with him those forms of civility which society prescribes, and feel far kinder to him than if we had shut the door in his face, and said, 'Go along, you tiresome fellow!' Now why does not this very obvious philosophy apply to better and higher feelings? The forms of religion are as much more necessary than the forms of politeness and social good-will as religion is more important than all other things."

"Besides," said my wife, "a form of worship, kept up from year to year in a family, — the assembling of parents and children for a few sacred moments each day, though it may be a form many times, especially in the gay and thoughtless hours of life, — often becomes invested with deep sacredness in times of trouble, or in those crises that rouse our deeper feelings. In sickness, in bereavement, in separation, the daily prayer at home has a sacred and healing power. Then we remember the scattered and wandering ones; and the scattered and wandering think tenderly of that hour when they know they are remembered. I know, when I was a young girl, I was often thoughtless and careless about family-prayers; but now that my father and mother are gone forever, there is nothing I recall more often. I remember the great old Family Bible, the hymn-book, the chair where father used to sit. I see him as he looked bending over that Bible more than in any other way; and expressions and sentences in his prayers which fell unheeded on my ears in those days have often come back to me like comforting angels. We are not aware of the influence things are having on us till we have left them far behind in years. When we have summered and wintered them, and look back on them from changed times and other days, we find that they were making their mark upon us, though we knew it not."

"I have often admired," said I, "the stateliness and regularity of family-worship in good old families in England, — the servants, guests, and children all assembled, — the reading of the Scriptures and the daily prayers by the master or mistress of the family, ending with the united repetition of the Lord's Prayer by all."

14

"No such assemblage is possible in our country," said Bob. "Our servants are for the most part Roman Catholics, and forbidden by their rèligion to join with us in acts of worship."

"The greater the pity," said I. "It is a pity that all Christians who can conscientiously, repeat the Apostles' Creed and the Lord's Prayer together should for any reason be forbidden to do so. It would do more to harmonize our families, and promote good feeling between masters and servants, to meet once a day on the religious ground common to both, than many sermons on reciprocal duties."

"But while the case is so," said Marianne, "we can't help it. Our servants cannot unite with us; our daily prayers are something forbidden to them."

"We cannot in this country," said I, "give to family prayer that solemn stateliness which it has in a country where religion is a civil institution, and masters and servants, as a matter of course, belong to one church. Our prayers must resemble more a private interview with a father than a solemn act of homage to a king. They must be more intimate and domestic. The hour of family devotion should be the children's hour, — held dear as the interval when the busy father drops his business and cares, and, like Jesus of old, takes the little ones in his arms and blesses them. The child should remember

it as the time when the father always seemed most
accessible and loving. The old family .worship of
New England lacked this character of domesticity and
intimacy, — it was stately and formal, distant and
cold ; but whatever were its defects, I cannot think
it an improvement to leave it out altogether, as too
many good sort of people in our day are doing. There
may be practical religion where its outward daily
forms are omitted, but there is assuredly no more of it
for the omission. No man loves God and his neighbor
less, is a *less* honest and good man, for daily prayers
in his household, — the chances are quite the other
way; and if the spirit of love rules the family hour,
it may prove the source and spring of all that is
good through the day. It seems to be a solemn duty
in the parents thus to make the Invisible Father-
hood real to their children, who can receive this idea
at first only through outward forms and observances.
The little one thus learns that his father has a Father
in heaven, and that the earthly life he is living is only a sacrament and emblem, — a type of the eternal
life which infolds it, and of more lasting relations there.
Whether, therefore, it be the silent grace and silent
prayer of the Friends, or the form of prayer of ritual
churches, or the extemporaneous outpouring of those
whose habits and taste lead them to extempore prayer,
— in one of these ways there should be daily outward and visible acts of worship in every family."

"Well, now," said Bob, "about this old question of Sunday-keeping, Marianne and I are much divided. I am always for doing something that she thinks is n't the thing."

"Well, you see," said Marianne, "Bob is always talking against our old Puritan fathers, and saying all manner of hard things about them. He seems to think that all their ways and doings must of course have been absurd. For my part, I don't think we are in any danger of being too strict about anything. It appears to me that in this country there is a general tendency to let all sorts of old forms and observances float down-stream, and yet nobody seems quite to have made up his mind what shall come next."

"The fact is," said I, "that we realize very fully all the objections and difficulties of the experiments in living that we have tried; but the difficulties in others that we are intending to try have not yet come to light. The Puritan Sabbath had great and very obvious evils. Its wearisome restraints and over-strictness cast a gloom on religion, and arrayed against the day itself the active prejudices that now are undermining it and threatening its extinction. But it had great merits and virtues, and produced effects on society that we cannot well afford to dispense with. The clearing of a whole day from all possibilities of labor and amusement necessarily produced a grave and thoughtful people; and a democratic republic can be carried on by no other. In lands which have Sabbaths of mere amusement, mere gala-days, republics rise and fall as fast as children's card-houses; and the reason is, they are built by those whose political and religious education has been childish. The common people of Europe have been sedulously nursed on amusements by the reigning powers, to keep them from meddling with serious matters; their religion has been sensuous and sentimental, and their Sabbaths thoughtless holidays. The common people of New England are educated to think, to reason, to examine all questions of politics and religion for themselves; and one deeply thoughtful day every week baptizes and strengthens their reflective and reasoning faculties. The Sunday schools of Paris are whirligigs where Young France rides round and round on little hobby-horses till his brain spins even faster than Nature made it to spin; and when he grows up, his political experiments are as whirligig as his Sunday education. If I were to choose between the Sabbath of France and the old Puritan Sabbath, I should hold up both hands for the latter, with all its objectionable features."

"Well," said my wife, "cannot we contrive to retain all that is really valuable of the Sabbath, and to ameliorate and smooth away what is forbidding?"

" That is the problem of our day," said I.   " We do not want the Sabbath of Continental Europe : it does not suit democratic institutions ; it cannot be made even a quiet or a safe day, except by means of that ever-present armed police that exists there.   If the Sabbath of America is simply to be a universal loafing, pic-nicking, dining-out day, as it is now with all our foreign population, we shall need what they have in Europe, the gendarmes at every turn, to protect the fruit on our trees and the melons in our fields.   People who live a little out from great cities see enough, and more than enough, of this sort of Sabbath-keeping, with our loose American police.

" The fact is, our system of government was organ-ized to go by moral influences as much as mills by water, and Sunday was the great day for concentrat-ing these influences and bringing them to bear ; and we might just as well break down all the dams and let out all the water of the Lowell mills, and expect still to work the looms, as to expect to work our laws and constitution with European notions of religion.

" It is true the Puritan Sabbath had its disagreeable points.   So have the laws of Nature.   They are of a most uncomfortable sternness and rigidity ; yet for all that, we would hardly join in a petition to have them repealed, or made wavering and uncertain for human convenience.   We can bend to them in a thousand ways, and live very comfortably under them."

" But," said Bob, " Sabbath-keeping is the iron rod of bigots ; they don't allow a man any liberty of his own. One says it's wicked to write a letter Sunday ; another holds that you must read no book but the Bible ; and a third is scandalized, if you take a walk, ever so quietly, in the fields. There are all sorts of quips and turns. We may fasten things with pins of a Sunday, but it's wicked to fasten with needle and thread, and so on, and so on ; and each one, planting himself on his own individual mode of keeping Sunday, points his guns and frowns severely over the battlements on his neighbors whose opinions and practice are different from his."

"Yet," said I, " Sabbath-days are expressly mentioned by Saint Paul as among those things concerning which no man should judge another. It seems to me that the error as regards the Puritan Sabbath was in representing it, not as a gift from God to man, but as a tribute of man to God. Hence all these hagglings and nice questions and exactions to the uttermost farthing. The holy time must be weighed and measured. It must begin at twelve o'clock of one night, and end at twelve o'clock of another ; and from beginning to end, the mind must be kept in a state of tension by the effort not to think any of its usual thoughts or do any of its usual works. The fact is, that the metaphysical, defining, hair-splitting mind of New England, turning its whole powers on this one bit of ritual, this one only day of divine service, which was left of all the feasts and fasts of the old churches, made of it a thing straiter and stricter than ever the old Jews dreamed of.

"The old Jewish Sabbath entered only into the physical region, merely enjoining cessation from physical toil. 'Thou shalt not *labor* nor do any *work*,' covered the whole ground. In other respects than this it was a joyful festival, resembling, in the mode of keeping it, the Christmas of the modern Church. It was a day of social hilarity, — the Jewish law strictly forbidding mourning and gloom during festivals. The people were commanded on feast-days to rejoice before the Lord their God with all their might. We fancy there were no houses where children were afraid to laugh, where the voice of social cheerfulness quavered away in terror lest it should awake a wrathful God. The Jewish Sabbath was instituted, in the absence of printing, of books, and of all the advantages of literature, to be the great means of preserving sacred history, — a day cleared from all possibility of other employment than social and family communion, when the heads of families and the elders of tribes might instruct the young in those religious traditions which have thus come down to us.

"The Christian Sabbath is meant to supply the

same moral need in that improved and higher state of society which Christianity introduced. Thus it was changed from the day representing the creation of the world to the resurrection-day of Him who came to make all things new. The Jewish Sabbath was buried with Christ in the sepulchre, and arose with Him, not a Jewish, but a Christian festival, still holding in itself that provision for man's needs which the old institution possessed, but with a wider and more generous freedom of application. It was given to the Christian world as a day of rest, of refreshment, of hope and joy, — and of worship. The manner of making it such a day was left open and free to the needs and convenience of the varying circumstances and characters of those for whose benefit it was instituted."

"Well," said Bob, " don't you think there is a deal of nonsense about Sabbath-keeping?"

"There is a deal of nonsense about everything human beings have to deal with," said I.

"And," said Marianne, "how to find out what is nonsense?"

"By clear conceptions," said I, "of what the day is for. I should define the Sabbath as a divine and fatherly gift to man, — a day expressly set apart for the cultivation of his moral nature. Its object is not merely physical rest and recreation, but moral im-

provement. The former are proper to the day only
so far as they are subservient to the latter. The
whole human race have the conscious need of being
made better, purer, and more spiritual ; the whole
human race have one common danger of sinking to a
mere animal life under the pressure of labor or in the
dissipations of pleasure ; and of the whole human race
the proverb holds good, that what may be done any
time is done at no time.   Hence the Heavenly Father
appoints one day as a special season for the culture of
man's highest faculties.   Accordingly, whatever ways
and practices interfere with the purpose of the Sabbath as a day of worship and moral culture should
be avoided ; and all family arrangements for the day
should be made with reference thereto."

"Cold dinners on Sunday, for example," said Bob.
"Marianne holds these as prime articles of faith."

"Yes, — they doubtless are most worthy and merciful, in giving to the poor cook one day she may call
her own, and rest from the heat of range and cooking-
stove.   For the same reason, I would suspend as far as
possible all travelling, and all public labor, on Sunday.
The hundreds of hands that these things require to
carry them on are the hands of human beings, whose
right to this merciful pause of rest is as clear as their
humanity.   Let them have their day to look upward."

"But the little ones," said my oldest matron daughter, who had not as yet spoken, — "they are the problem. Oh, this weary labor of making children keep Sunday! If I try it, I have no rest at all myself. If I must talk to them or read to them to keep them from play, my Sabbath becomes my hardest working-day."

"And, pray, what commandment of the Bible ever said children should not play on Sunday?" said I. "We are forbidden to work, and we see the reason why; but lambs frisk and robins sing on Sunday; and little children, who are as yet more than half animals, must not be made to keep the day in the manner proper to our more developed faculties. As much cheerful, attractive religious instruction as they can bear without weariness may be given, and then they may simply be restrained from disturbing others. Say to the little one, — 'This day we have noble and beautiful things to think of that interest us deeply; you are a child; you cannot read and think and enjoy such things as much as we can; you may play softly and quietly, and remember not to make a disturbance.' I would take a child to public worship at least once of a Sunday; it forms a good habit in him. If the sermon be long and unintelligible, there are the little Sabbath-school books in every child's hands; and while the grown people are getting what they understand, who shall forbid a child's getting what is suited to

him in a way that interests him and disturbs nobody?
The Sabbath school is the child's church; and happily
it is yearly becoming a more and more attractive institution. I approve the custom of those who beautify
the Sabbath school-room with plants, flowers, and
pictures, thus making it an attractive place to the
childish eye. The more this custom prevails, the
more charming in after years will be the memories
of Sunday.

"It is most especially to be desired that the whole
air and aspect of the day should be one of cheerfulness. Even the new dresses, new bonnets, and
new shoes, in which children delight of a Sunday,
should not be despised. They have their value in
marking the day as a festival; and it is better for
the child to long for Sunday for the sake of his little
new shoes than that he should hate and dread it as
a period of wearisome restraint. All the latitude
should be given to children that can be, consistently
with fixing in their minds the idea of a sacred season. I would rather that the atmosphere of the day
should resemble that of a weekly Thanksgiving than
that it should make its mark on the tender mind
only by the memory of deprivations and restrictions."

"Well," said Bob, "here's Marianne always breaking her heart about my reading on Sunday. Now I

hold that what is bad on Sunday is bad on Monday,
— and what is good on Monday is good on Sunday."

"We cannot abridge other people's liberty," said I.
"The generous, confiding spirit of Christianity has
imposed not a single restriction upon us in reference
to Sunday. The day is put at our disposal as a good
Father hands a piece of money to his child : — 'There
it is; take it and spend it well.' The child knows
from his father's character what he means by spending it well; but he is left free to use his own judgment
as to the mode.

"If a man conscientiously feels that reading of this
or that description is the best for him as regards his
moral training and improvement, let him pursue it,
and let no man judge him. It is difficult, with the
varying temperaments of men, to decide what are or
are not religious books. One man is more religiously
impressed by the reading of history or astronomy than
he would be by reading a sermon. There may be
overwrought and wearied states of the brain and
nerves which require and make proper the diversions
of light literature; and if so, let it be used. The
mind must have its recreations as well as the body."

"But for children and young people," said my
daughter, — "would you let them read novels on
Sunday?"

"That is exactly like asking, Would you let them

talk with people on Sunday? Now people are different; it depends, therefore, on who they are. Some are trifling and flighty, some are positively bad-principled, some are altogether good in their influence. So of the class of books called novels. Some are merely frivolous, some are absolutely noxious and dangerous, others again are written with a strong moral and religious purpose, and, being vivid and interesting, produce far more religious effect on the mind than dull treatises and sermons. The parables of Christ sufficiently establish the point that there is no inherent objection to the use of fiction in teaching religious truth. Good religious fiction, thoughtfully read, may be quite as profitable as any other reading."

"But don't you think," said Marianne, "that there is danger in too much fiction?"

"Yes," said I. "But the chief danger of all that class of reading is its *easiness*, and the indolent, careless mental habits it induces. A great deal of the reading of young people on all days is really reading to no purpose, its object being merely present amusement. It is a listless yielding of the mind to be washed over by a stream which leaves no fertilizing properties, and carries away by constant wear the good soil of thought. I should try to establish a barrier against this kind of reading, not only on Sunday, but on Monday, on Tuesday, and on all days. Instead, therefore, of objecting to any particular class of books for Sunday reading, I should say in general, that reading merely for pastime, without any moral aim, is the thing to be guarded against. That which inspires no thought, no purpose, which steals away all our strength and energy, and makes the Sabbath a day of dreams, is the reading I would object to.

"So of music. I do not see the propriety of confining one's self to technical sacred music. Any grave, solemn, thoughtful, or pathetic music has a proper relation to our higher spiritual nature, whether it be printed in a church service-book or on secular sheets. On me, for example, Beethoven's Sonatas have a far more deeply religious influence than much that has religious names and words. Music is to be judged of by its effects."

"Well," said Bob, "if Sunday is given for our own individual improvement, I for one should not go to church. I think I get a great deal more good in staying at home and reading."

"There are two considerations to be taken into account in reference to this matter of church-going," I replied. "One relates to our duty as members of society in keeping up the influence of the Sabbath, and causing it to be respected in the community ; the other, to the proper disposition of our time for our own moral improvement. As members of the com-

munity, we should go to church, and do all in our
power to support the outward ordinances of religion.
If a conscientious man makes up his mind that Sunday is a day for outward acts of worship and reverence, he should do his own part as an individual
towards sustaining these observances.   Even though
he may have such mental and moral resources that
as an individual he could gain much more in solitude
than in a congregation, still he owes to the congregation the influence of his presence and sympathy.
But I have never yet seen the man, however finely
gifted morally and intellectually, whom I thought in
the long run a gainer in either of these respects by
the neglect of public worship.   I have seen many
who in their pride kept aloof from the sympathies
and communion of their brethren, who lost strength
morally, and deteriorated in ways that made themselves painfully felt.   Sunday is apt in such cases to
degenerate into a day of mere mental idleness and
reverie, or to become a sort of waste-paper box for
scraps, odds and ends of secular affairs.

"As to those very good people — and many such
there are — who go straight on with the work of life on
Sunday, on the plea that "to labor is to pray," I simply think they are mistaken.   In the first place, to
labor is *not* the same thing as to pray.   It may sometimes be as good a thing to do, and in some cases

even a better thing; but it is not the same thing. A man might as well never write a letter to his wife on the plea that making money for her is writing to her. It may possibly be quite as great a proof of love to work for a wife as to write to her, but few wives would not say that both were not better than either alone. Furthermore, there is no doubt that the intervention of one day of spiritual rest and aspiration so refreshes a man's whole nature, and oils the many wheels of existence, that he who allows himself a weekly Sabbath does more work in the course of his life for the omission of work on that day.

"A young student in a French college, where the examinations are rigidly severe, found by experience that he succeeded best in his examination by allowing one day of entire rest just before it. His brain and nervous system refreshed in this way carried him through the work better than if taxed to the last moment. There are men transacting a large and complicated business who can testify to the same influence from the repose of the Sabbath.

"I believe those Christian people who from conscience and principle turn their thoughts most entirely out of the current of worldly cares on Sunday fulfil unconsciously a great law of health; and that, whether their moral nature be thereby advanced or not, their brain will work more healthfully and actively for it even in physical and worldly matters. It is because the Sabbath thus harmonizes the physical and moral laws of our being, that the injunction concerning it is placed among the ten great commandments, each of which represents some one of the immutable needs of humanity.

"There is yet another point of family religion that ought to be thought of," said my wife : "I mean the customs of mourning. If there is anything that ought to distinguish Christian families from Pagans, it should be their way of looking at and meeting those inevitable events that must from time to time break the family chain. It seems to be the peculiarity of Christianity to shed hope on such events. And yet it seems to me as if it were the very intention of many of the customs of society to add tenfold to their gloom and horror, — such swathings of black crape, such funereal mufflings of every pleasant object, such darkening of rooms, and such seclusion from society and giving up to bitter thoughts and lamentation. How can little children that look on such things believe that there is a particle of truth in all they hear about the joyous and comforting doctrines which the Bible holds forth for such times?"

"That subject is a difficult one," I rejoined. "Nature seems to indicate a propriety in some outward expressions of grief when we lose our friends. All nations agree in these demonstrations. In a certain degree they are soothing to sorrow; they are the language of external life made to correspond to the internal. Wearing mourning has its advantages. It is a protection to the feelings of the wearer, for whom it procures sympathetic and tender consideration; it saves grief from many a hard jostle in the ways of life; it prevents the necessity of many a trying explanation, and is the ready apology for many an omission of those tasks to which sorrow is unequal. For all these reasons I never could join the crusade which some seem disposed to wage against it. Mourning, however, ought not to be continued for years. Its uses are more for the first few months of sorrow, when it serves the mourner as a safeguard from intrusion, insuring quiet and leisure, in which to reunite the broken threads of life, and to gather strength for a return to its duties. But to wear mourning garments and forego society for two or three years after the loss of any friend, however dear, I cannot but regard as a morbid, unhealthy nursing of sorrow, unworthy of a Christian."

"And yet," said my wife, " to such an unhealthy degree does this custom prevail, that I have actually known young girls who have never worn any other dress than mourning, and consequently never been into society, during the entire period of their girlhood.

First, the death of a father necessitated three years of funereal garments and abandonment of social relations ; then the death of a brother added two years more ; and before that mourning was well ended, another of a wide circle of relatives being taken, the habitual seclusion was still protracted. What must a child think of the Christian doctrine of life and death, who has never seen life except through black crape? We profess to believe in a better life to which the departed good are called, — to believe in the shortness of our separation, the certainty of reunion, and that all these events are arranged in all their relations by an infinite tenderness which cannot err. Surely, Christian funerals too often seem to say that affliction "cometh of the dust," and not from above.

"But," said Bob, "after all, death is a horror ; you can make nothing less of it. You can't smooth it over, nor dress it with flowers ; it is what Nature shudders at."

"It is precisely for this reason," said I, "that Christians should avoid those customs which aggravate and intensify this natural dread. Why overpower the senses with doleful and funereal images in the hour of weakness and bereavement, when the soul needs all her force to rise above the gloom of earth, and to realize the mysteries of faith? Why shut the friendly sunshine from the mourner's room? Why muffle in a white shroud every picture that speaks a cheerful household word to the eye? Why make a house look stiff and ghastly and cold as a corpse? In some of our cities, on the occurrence of a death in the family, all the shutters on the street are closed and tied with black crape, and so remain for months. What an oppressive gloom must this bring on a house! how like the very shadow of death! It is enlisting the nerves and the senses against our religion, and making more difficult the great duty of returning to life and its interests. I would have flowers and sunshine in the deserted rooms, and make them symbolical of the cheerful mansions above, to which our beloved ones are gone. Home ought to be so religiously cheerful, so penetrated by the life of love and hope and Christian faith, that the other world may be made real by it. Our home life should be a type of the higher life. Our home should be so sanctified, its joys and its sorrows so baptized and hallowed, that it shall not be sacrilegious to think of heaven as a higher form of the same thing, — a Father's house in the better country, whose mansions are many, whose love is perfect, whose joy is eternal."

Cambridge : Stereotyped and Printed by Welch, Bigelow, & Co.